NONTRADITIONAL CAREERS FOR WOMEN

It is no longer necessary for women to confine themselves to the traditional occupations of teacher, nurse, librarian, secretary or telephone operator. NONTRADITIONAL CAREERS FOR WOMEN, the first and only book of its kind, covers more than 500 nontraditional occupations which offer employment opportunities to women. This timely and valuable book discusses in detail careers in law, medicine, the healing arts, the helping professions, science and math, engineering, the creative arts, business, the manual trades and government services. Success and fulfillment await the intelligent, ambitious woman today. It need no longer be a "man's world" for those women with the abilities, interests and fortitude needed to break into fields formerly closed to them.

BOOKS BY SARAH SPLAVER

NONTRADITIONAL CAREERS FOR WOMEN

NONTRADITIONAL COLLEGE ROUTES TO CAREERS

PARAPROFESSIONS
Careers of the Future and the Present

YOU AND TODAY'S TROUBLED WORLD—A Psychologist
Talks to Urban Youth

YOUR CAREER—IF YOU'RE NOT GOING TO COLLEGE

YOUR COLLEGE EDUCATION—HOW TO PAY FOR IT

YOUR HANDICAP—DON'T LET IT HANDICAP YOU

YOUR PERSONALITY AND YOU

Nontraditional Careers for Women

by *SARAH SPLAVER, Ph.D.*

JULIAN MESSNER NEW YORK

Published by Julian Messner, a Division of Simon & Schuster, Inc.
1 West 39 Street, New York, N. Y. 10018. All rights reserved.

Fourth Printing, 1975

to
an exceptionally good and wise woman,
my mother,
a true traditionalist

Library of Congress Cataloging in Publication Data

Splaver, Sarah.
    Nontraditional careers for women.

    SUMMARY: Discusses over 500 careers for women in such fields
as law, medicine, science, math, engineering, creative arts, business,
manual trades, and government services.
    Bibliography: p. 222
    1. Vocational guidance for women—Juvenile literature.
[1. Vocational guidance]   I. Title.
HF5381.2.S59   331.7′02   73-5384
ISBN 0-671-32619-8
ISBN 0-671-32620-1 (lib. bdg.)

Printed in the United States of America

ACKNOWLEDGMENT

The author conducted a comprehensive research study to obtain the very latest authoritative information on the new, expanding opportunities for women in the vast gamut of male-dominated occupations. Questionnaires and letters of inquiry were sent to more than a thousand professional associations, labor unions, educational and miscellaneous other institutions, industrial organizations, corporations, government agencies, a miscellany of women's organizations, caucuses, committees and other women's groups and just about every other conceivable entity involved with the employment of women in nontraditional fields. Where necessary, there were follow-up letters, telephone communications and personal interviews. With the exception of some of the trade unions, whose reactions at best were lukewarm, the over-all response was excellent. The author wishes to express her heartfelt thanks to all who wholeheartedly cooperated and offered their invaluable time and assistance to help make this book as thoroughly all-encompassing and up-to-date as possible and is sorry that space limitations make it impossible to list their names.

Included in this book are brief "success tales" of women who accomplished the difficult task of overcoming the obstacles and succeeding in careers long considered nontraditional for women. The author expresses her most sincere thanks and grateful appreciation to the following "women of achievement" for their gracious cooperation and permission to be quoted: Helen M. Free (Chairman, Women Chemists Committee, American Chemical Society), New Products Manager, Clinical Test Systems, Ames Company, Division of Miles Laboratories, Inc., Elkhart, Ind. 46514; Dr. Jean D. Gibbons (Chairperson, Committee on Women in Statistics, American Statistical Association), Professor and Chairman, Department of Statistics and Quantitative Methods, University of Alabama, College of Commerce and Business Ad-

5

Acknowledgment

ministration, University, Ala. 35486; Dr. Bonnie V. Gustafson (President, Women's Veterinary Medical Association), Texas A & M University, College of Veterinary Medicine, Department of Veterinary Anatomy, College Station, Tex. 77843; Dr. Frances Keller Harding (Immediate Past President, American Medical Women's Association), Obstetrician-Gynecologist, Columbus, Ohio, 43224; NettaBell Girard Larson (President, National Association of Women Lawyers), Attorney, Larson and Larson, Law Firm, Riverton, Wyo. 82501; Dr. Essie E. Lee, Director of Student Affairs, Division of Student Services, Institute of Health Sciences, Hunter College of the City University of New York, New York, N.Y. 10029; Naomi J. McAfee (President, Society of Women Engineers), Manager, Quality and Reliability Assurance, Westinghouse Electric Corporation, Defense and Electronic Systems Center, Baltimore, Md. 21203; Joan Murray, Television News Correspondent, Columbia Broadcasting System, and Executive Vice-President, ZEBRA Associates, Inc., New York, N.Y. 10022; Lillian D. Rock (Cofounder, International Federation of Women Lawyers), Senior Member, Rock and Rock, Law Firm, New York, N.Y. 10017; Wilma C. Rogalin, Senior Manager, Women's Opportunities (formerly Personnel Manager), Pan American World Airways, New York, N.Y. 10017.

The author also wishes to express her sincere appreciation to Russell B. Flanders, Chief, Division of Manpower and Occupational Outlook, Bureau of Labor Statistics, U.S. Department of Labor, Washington, D.C. 20212, and Elizabeth Duncan Koontz, Deputy Assistant Secretary of Labor and Director, Women's Bureau, U.S. Department of Labor, Washington, D.C. 20210.

To her ever-faithful "Washington representatives," Eve and Al Chaiken, for their ever-competent assistance, the author offers particular thanks and grateful appreciation. Special thanks go too to Nathaniel L. Rock for his wise and invaluable legal counsel.

S. S.

CONTENTS

1. THE WORKING WAYS OF WOMEN   25
   Then and Now   25
   From Female Fables to Facts   26
   Now and New   28
   Where the Action Is   29

2. PORTIAS IN THE LEGAL FIELD   32
   Lawyers (Attorneys, Counselors at Law)   33
   Criminal Lawyers   34
   Civil Lawyers   34
      Corporation Lawyers   34
      Divorce Lawyers   35
      Labor Lawyers   35
      Negligence Lawyers   35
      Patent Lawyers   35
      Probate Lawyers   35
      Real Estate Lawyers   35
   Legal Aid Society Lawyers   37
   Public Defenders   37
   Corporation Counsels (Solicitors)   40
      Assistant Corporation Counsels   40
   Attorneys-General   40
      Assistant Attorneys-General   40
   District Attorneys (Prosecutors)   40
      Assistant District Attorneys   40
   Judges   43
   Magistrates   43
   Supreme Court Justices   43

   Legal Paraprofessionals (Legal Assistants)   45

Contents

3. FEMALE PHYSICIANS AND SURGEONS   46
   Physicians (Medical Doctors)   46
   Interns   50
   General Practitioners   50
   Resident Physicians (Residents)   50
   Medical Specialists   50
     Pediatricians   50
     Surgeons   51
       Orthopedic Surgeons   51
       Heart Surgeons   51
       Plastic Surgeons   51
     Internists   51
       Cardiologists   52
     Psychiatrists   52
     Family Physicians   53
     Anesthesiologists   53
     Pathologists   53
     Obstetricians   53
     Gynecologists   53
     Dermatologists   55
     Neurologists   55
     Ophthalmologists   55
     Otolaryngologists   55
     Radiologists   55
     Plastic Surgeons   55
     Aerospace Medicine Specialists   55

     Medical paraprofessionals (Physician's Assistants)   57

4. THE HEALING ARTS   58
   Registered Nurses   58
   Licensed Practical Nurses   58

   Dentists   58
     Orthodontists   59
     Exodontists   59
     Pedodontists   59
     Periodontists   59

Contents

Prosthodontists 59
Dental Laboratory Technicians 60
Dental Hygienists 61
Dental Assistants 61

Osteopathic Physicians 62
Veterinarians 62
Chiropractors 65
Optometrists 66
Optical Mechanics (Optical Laboratory Technicians) 68
Dispensing Opticians 68
Pharmacists 69
  Retail Pharmacists 71
  Hospital Pharmacists 71
  Medical Sales Representatives ("Detail Men") 71
Podiatrists (Chiropodists) 72
Hospital Administrators 73
  Assistant Hospital Administrators 74
Sanitarians (Environmentalists) 74
Inhalation Therapists (Oxygen Therapy Technicians) 75

EEG Technicians (Electroencephalographic Technicians) 76
EKG Technicians (Electrocardiographic Technicians) 77
Occupational Therapists 77
Physical Therapists 77
Radiological Technologists (Medical X-Ray Technicians) 77
Medical Assistants 78
Medical Laboratory Workers 78
Medical Technologists 78
Medical Record Librarians 78
Medical Librarians 78
Dietitians 79
Speech Pathologists 79
Audiologists 79

Contents

5. THE HELPING PROFESSIONS   81
   Teachers   81
     Kindergartners   81
     Elementary School Teachers   81
     Teachers of Handicapped Children   82
     Teachers of Mentally Retarded   82
     Teachers of Disadvantaged Children 82
     Secondary School Teachers   82
       Junior High School Teachers   82
       Senior High School Teachers   82
       Physical Science Teachers   82
   District Superintendents   83
   School Administrators   83
   Principals   83

   School Counselors (Guidance Counselors)   83
   Adjustment Counselors   83
   Advisers   84
   Directors of Guidance   84
   Grade Advisers   84
   College Advisers (Secondary School Level) 84
   Placement Counselors   84
   Supervisors of Guidance   85
   Student Personnel Specialists   88
     Directors of Student Affairs   88
     Admissions Officers   88
     Directors of Admissions   88
     College Advisers (College and University Level) 88
     Financial Aid Officers   88
     Directors of Financial Aid   88
     College Placement Officers (College Career
       Planning and Placement Counselors) 88

   College and University Faculty Members (College
     Teachers)   89
   Lecturers   89
   Instructors   89
   Assistant Professors   89

Associate Professors 89
Full Professors 89

Employment Counselors (Vocational Counselors) 91
Rehabilitation Counselors 92
Social Workers 93
  Caseworkers 94
  Group Workers 94
  Medical Social Workers 94
  Psychiatric Social Workers 94
  School Social Workers 94
Psychologists 94
  Clinical Psychologists 95
  Counseling Psychologists 95
  Experimental Psychologists 95
  Industrial Psychologists 95
  School Psychologists 95
  Social Psychologists 95

Social Scientists 97
  Anthropologists 97
  Economists 97
  Geographers 98
  Historians 98
  Political Scientists 98
  Sociologists 98

Mental Health Paraprofessionals 99
  Mental Health Technicians 99
  Human Services Technicians 99
Art Therapists 100
Music Therapists 100

Members of the Clergy 100
  Clergywomen 101
  Protestant Ministers 101
  Pastor's Assistants 101
  Roman Catholic Priests 101
  Rabbis 102

Contents

6. WOMEN IN MATH AND SCIENCE   103

  Mathematicians   104
    Theoretical Mathematicians   104
    Applied Mathematicians   104
  Actuaries   105
  Statisticians   106

  Environmental Scientists   109
    Geologists   109
    Geophysicists   109
      Geodesists   109
      Seismologists   109
    Meteorologists   109
      Weather Forecasters   110
    Oceanographers   110

  Life Scientists   112
    Biologists (Biological Scientists)   112
    Botanists   112
      Plant Ecologists   112
      Plant Morphologists   112
      Plant Pathologists   112
      Plant Physiologists   112
      Plant Taxonomists   112
    Zoologists   112
      Herpetologists   112
      Ichthyologists   112
      Mammalogists   112
      Ornithologists   112
    Microbiologists   112
      Bacteriologists   112
      Virologists   112
    Agronomists   113
    Anatomists   113
      Cytologists   113
      Histologists   113

Contents

Biochemists 113
Biological Oceanographers (Aquatic Biologists) 114
Biophysicists 114
Ecologists 114
    Animal Ecologists 114
    Plant Ecologists 114
Embryologists 114
Entomologists 114
    Apiculturists 114
Foresters 114
Geneticists 115
    Plant Breeders 115
    Animal Breeders 115
Horticulturists 115
    Floriculturists 115
    Olericulturists 115
    Pomologists 115
Husbandry Specialists 115
    Animal Husbandmen 115
    Dog Breeders 115
    Cattle Ranchers 115
Nutritionists 115
Pharmacologists 115
Physiologists 116

Physical Scientists 118
Chemists 118
    Industrial Chemists 119
    Inorganic Chemists 119
    Organic Chemists 119
    Research Chemists 119
Physicists 123
    Acoustics Physicists 123
    Atomic and Molecular Physicists 123
    Nuclear Physicists 123
Astronomers 125
Food Scientists (Food Technologists) 126

Contents

7. ENGINEERING WOMEN HAVE FAST-GROWING
   FUTURES   128
   Engineers   129
     Electrical Engineers   130
     Electronics Engineers   130
     Mechanical Engineers   130
     Civil Engineers   131
       Highway Engineers   131
     Industrial Engineers   131
     Aerospace Engineers   131
     Chemical Engineers   131
     Computer Engineers   132
     Agricultural Engineers   132
     Biomedical Engineers   132
     Ceramic Engineers   132
     Metallurgical Engineers   132
     Mining Engineers   132
     Nuclear Engineers   132

   Technicians   139
     Draftswomen   139
     Aeronautical and Aerospace Technicians   139
     Agricultural Technicians   139
     Air-Conditioning, Heating and Refrigeration
       Technicians   140
     Automotive Technicians   140
     Chemical Technicians   140
     Civil Engineering Technicians   140
     Computer Technicians   140
     Ecology Technicians   140
     Electronics Technicians   140
     Industrial Technicians   140
     Instrumentation Technicians   140
     Mechanical Technicians   140
       Diesel Technicians   140
       Machine Designers   140
       Tool Designers   140

Metallurgical Technicians 140
Meteorological Technicians 141
Nuclear Engineering Technicians 141
Radio and Television Broadcasting Technicians 141
Safety Technicians 141

Architects 142
Architectural Technicians 144
Urban Planners 144
Urban Planning Technicians 144
Landscape Architects 146
Surveyors 147

8. WRITING, CREATING AND COMMUNICATING 149
Writers 150
Authors 150
Novelists 150
Playwrights (Dramatists) 150
Short Story Writers 150
Free-Lance Article Writers 150
Poets 150
Songwriters (Lyricists) 150
Greeting Card Writers 151
Book Editors 154
Journalists 154
Editors 154
Financial Editors 154
Newspaper Reporters 154
Feature Reporters 154
Newspaper Correspondents 154
Foreign Correspondents 155
Columnists 155
Fashion Columnists 155
Political Columnists 155
Sports Columnists 155
Technical Writers 156
Science Writers 156

Contents

Medical Writers 156

Librarians 157

Painters 157

  Portrait Painters 158

  Watercolor Painters 158

Art Teachers 159

Commercial Artists (Illustrators) 159

  Advertising Artists 159

  Letterers 159

  Designers 159

    Book Designers 159

    Magazine Designers 159

    Package Designers 159

    Record Jacket Designers 160

  Greeting Card Artists 160

  Sign Painters 160

  Display Artists 160

  Window Trimmers 160

  Cartoonists 160

  Comic Strip Artists 160

Industrial Designers (Product Designers) 161

Interior Designers 162

Interior Decorators 162

Fashion Designers 163

Floral Designers 163

Beauticians (Cosmetologists) 163

Hairdressers 163

Photographers 164

  Aerial Photographers 164

  Commercial Photographers 164

  Industrial Photographers 164

  Motion Picture Photographers 164

  Portrait Photographers 164

  Press Photographers (Photojournalists) 164

Performers 165

  Actresses 165

Contents

Professional Dancers 166
Musicians 166
    Drummers 166
    Pianists 166
    Violinists 166
    Singers (Vocalists) 166
Motion Picture Narrators (Motion-Picture
    Commentators) 166
Motion Picture Projectionists (Cinematographers) 166
Scenario Writers 166
Motion Picture Directors 166
Motion Picture Producers 166
Radio and Television Broadcasting Personnel 167
    Announcers 167
    Continuity Writers 167
    Directors 167
        Associate Directors 167
    Film Editors 167
    Makeup Artists 167
    Newscasters 167
    Newswriters 167
    News Correspondents 167
    Program Assistants 170
    Program Directors 170
    Radio Engineers (Station Engineers) 170
    Radio and Television Producers 170
    Scenic Designers 170
    Script Writers 170
    Sound Effects Technicians 170

Professional Athletes 171
    Professional Baseball Players 171
    Professional Football Players 171
    Professional Golfers 172
    Professional Tennis Players 172
Coaches 172
Umpires 172

Contents

9. THE BUSINESS WORLD   173

  Office Workers   173

    Clerical Workers   173

    Stenographers   173

    Secretaries   173

    Bookkeeping Workers   173

    Cashiers   173

    Typists   173

    Telephone Operators   173

    Office Machine Operators   173

    Receptionists   173

  Personnel Workers   174

    Personnel Assistants   175

    Personnel Clerks   175

    Personnel Recruiters   175

    Personnel Interviewers   175

    Psychometricians (Psychological Testers)   175

    Training Assistants   175

    Training Specialists   175

    Employee Counselors   175

    Employee Relations Specialists   175

    Labor Relations Specialists   175

  Personnel Supervisors   175

  Assistant Personnel Directors   175

  Personnel Managers (Personnel Directors)   175

  Aviation Workers   178

    Reservation Clerks   178

    Ticket Agents   178

    Traffic Agents   178

    Airline Stewardesses   178

    Pilots and Copilots   178

    Flight Engineers   178

    Airline Dispatchers   178

      Assistant Dispatchers   178

    Ground Radio Operators and Teletypists   178

    FAA Air Traffic Controllers   179

    FAA Electronic Technicians   179

FAA Engineers 179
FAA Flight Standards Inspectors 179

Railroad Workers 180
  Brakemen 180
  Conductors 180
  Locomotive Engineers 180
  Locomotive Firemen 180

Bus Drivers 180
Taxi Drivers 180
Truck Drivers 180

Travel Agents 181
Travel Agency Owners 181
Assistant Hotel Managers 181
Hotel Managers 181
Motel Managers 181

Accountants 182
  Certified Public Accountants (CPAs) 182
  Tax Accountants 182
  Auditors 182
Bank Clerks 183
Bank Tellers 183
Bank Officers 184

Electronic Computer Operating Personnel 185
  Console and Auxiliary Equipment Operators 185
  Computer Operators 185
  Keypunch Operators 185
Computer Programers 185
Systems Analysts 186

Salespeople 187
  Retail Salespeople (Saleswomen) 187
    Furniture Salespeople 188
    Automobile Salespeople 188
    Automobile Parts Counterwomen 189
    Gasoline Service Station Attendants (Automobile Service Station Salespeople) 189

Contents

Wholesale Salespeople	189
Manufacturers' Salespeople (Manufacturers' Sales Representatives)	190
Sales Engineers	190
Securities Salespeople (Customers' Brokers)	190
Real Estate Brokers	191
Real Estate Salespeople	192
Real Estate Agents	192
Realtors	192
Insurance Agents	192
Insurance Brokers	192
Agent-Trainees	193
Claims Adjusters	194
Underwriters	194
Underwriting Trainees	194
Junior Underwriters	194
Advertising Workers	195
Advertising Managers	195
Account Executives	195
Copywriters	195
Layout Artists	195
Advertising Artists	195
Media Directors	196
Space Buyers	196
Time Buyers	196
Space Sellers	196
Time Sellers	196
Market Research Workers	196
Public Relations Workers	196
Press Agents	196
Promotion Managers	196
Public Relations Women	196
Publicity Directors	196
Managers-Executives	197
Departmental Managers	197
Business Managers	197

Entry-Level Management Personnel 197
  Manager-Trainees 197
  Administrative Assistants 197
  Junior Executives 197
  Supervisors 197
Middle-Level Managers 197
  Production Managers 197
  Purchasing Managers 197
  Sales Managers 197
Top-Level Managers 197
  Corporation Presidents 197
  Vice-Presidents 197
  Corporate Executives 197
Self-Employed Business Proprietors 198

10. WOMEN IN MANUAL TRADES 200
Craftsmen-Craftswomen 201
  Bricklayers 202
  Carpenters 202
  Cement Masons 202
  Construction Electricians 202
  Floor Covering Installers 202
  Glaziers 202
  Lathers 202
  Operating Engineers (Construction Machinery
    Operators) 202
  Painters and Paperhangers 202
  Plumbers and Pipefitters 202
  Roofers 202
  Sheet-Metal Workers 202

Mechanics-Repairmen 202
  Air-Conditioning, Refrigeration and Heating
    Mechanics 202
  Aircraft Mechanics 203
  Appliance Servicemen 203
  Automobile Body Repairmen 203
  Automobile Mechanics 203

Contents

Business Machine Servicemen 203
Diesel Mechanics 203
Furniture Upholsterers 203
Industrial Machinery Repairmen (Maintenance
  Mechanics) 203
Instrument Repairmen 203
Maintenance Electricians (Electrical Repairmen) 203
Television and Radio Service Technicians 203
Tool and Die Makers 203
Watch Repairmen (Watchmakers) 203

Telephone and PBX Installers and Repairmen 204
Central Office Craftsmen 204
Linemen and Cable Splicers 204

Apprentices 204
Journeymen-Journeywomen 205
Repairwomen 205
Servicewomen 205

11. THE GOVERNMENT SERVICES 207
Federal Government Employees 207
Civil Service Employees 207

Armed Security Guards 208
Postal Service Guards 208
Postal Service Mail Carriers 208

FBI Special Agents (G-Women) 208

Customs Inspectors 208
Customs Patrol Officers 208
Customs Security Officers 208
Import Specialists 208
Special Agents (Bureau of Customs) 208

State Department Security Officers 209
State Department Couriers 209
State Department Foreign Service Officers 209

Internal Revenue Agents 209
IRS Criminal Investigators 209

Servicewomen   210
    U. S. Army Brigadier Generals   210
    U. S. Air Force Generals   210
    U. S. Navy Admirals   210
    WAC DIs (Drill Instructors)   210
    Missile-Repair Crewmen   211
    Radar Technicians   211
    Electronics Specialists   211
    Heavy Equipment Operators   211

Policewomen–Police Officers   211
    Patrolwomen   212
    Detectives (Plainclotheswomen)   212
    Traffic Policewomen   212
    Police Sergeants   212
    Police Lieutenants   212
    Police Captains   212
  Superintendents   212
  Wardens   212

Firefighters   212

Politicians   213
Elected Officials   213
    President of the United States   213
    Vice-Presidents   213
    Councilwomen   213
    Assemblywomen   213
    State Senators   214
    Mayors   214
    Governors   214
    Congresswomen   214

12. STAMP OUT OUTMODED STEREOTYPES   216
  Women Are People   216
  If You Believe You Can Achieve, You Can!   217
  Eliminate Stereotypical Thinking   219

SUGGESTED FURTHER READINGS   222

Chapter 1

THE WORKING WAYS
OF WOMEN

YOU are a fortunate female. Yes—you are very fortunate, for you are among the first females to have the precious privilege of being able to use your intellect, talents, abilities and ambition to become just about whatever you wish.

It was not always thus. As a matter of fact, this privilege is of only very recent vintage. Many occupational options are open to you which were barred to your grandmothers and your mother.

Then and Now
Until quite recently, women were limited to a circumscribed circle of occupations.

Young women who went to college and wanted to enter the professions generally became teachers, librarians, nurses, social workers and dietitians. Young women who did not go to college tended to become office workers, secretaries, retail saleswomen and telephone operators. Many a female college graduate had to start as a secretary to gain entry into the field for which she had been trained at college. No employer would dare insist to a male college graduate that he work as a secretary before he would be permitted to do the work for which he had studied!

There is absolutely nothing wrong with being a teacher, librarian, nurse, social worker, dietitian, office worker, secretary, retail saleswoman or telephone operator. These are honorable occupations. But there is something very wrong with keeping female talents fenced in within a small cluster of occupations.

Fifty years ago, the average woman worker was single and twenty-eight years old. In 1970, she was married and thirty-nine years of age. In 1920, only 23 per cent of all women between the ages of eighteen and sixty-five were in the labor force. Fifty years later, 50 per cent were working, and this percentage is rising rapidly.

In 1970, women represented 51 per cent of the population of the United States and approximately 40 per cent of our labor force. Yet women represented less than 1 per cent of the engineers of this country, only 1 per cent of the dentists, 2 per cent of the pharmacists, 3 per cent of the lawyers and 7 per cent of the physicians. This contrasts with the fact that in the Soviet Union, women represented 28 per cent of their engineers, 83 per cent of their dentists, 95 per cent of their pharmacists, 36 per cent of their lawyers and 75 per cent of their physicians.

False labels and job fables have kept women tied to traditional stereotypic occupations. The false labels on occupations, such as "male-only" and "female-only," are now illegal according to recent Federal legislation which bars discrimination on the basis of sex. Job fables have made women appear incapable of performing so many tasks they can very well do.

Discrimination against women has caused the underutilization of female talents and thus impeded not just the progress of women but also the vast potential of our nation. If the United States of America is to remain a great power, we can no longer afford to waste female brainpower.

From Female Fables to Facts

There was a time when women filled a tub with water and washed the family laundry in it, got down on their hands and knees and scrubbed the floors, baked loaves of bread for a large family and truly kept the home fires burning by putting coals into the belly stove in the kitchen.

Gone are the washtubs, scrub brushes, belly stoves, homemade bread, large families and a great deal more that kept our grandmothers totally occupied as housewives. In their place are the timesaving and energy-saving washing machines and dryers, vacuum cleaners and floor waxers, ready-made mass-produced breads and other foods, automatic heating systems and a vast variety of technological advances which have made of modern housewifery much less than a "total occupation."

Those who would like to keep women "in their place" (an expression used too in reference to Blacks, American Indians, Chicanos, Jews, Catholics and other persecuted minorities) try to perpetuate the fable that homemaking is a full-time job. The fact is that it is not. Technology and labor-saving equipment have eliminated much of the work done around the house by the housewife of yore. So much of what was formerly produced in the home is now available in the supermarkets or elsewhere.

All too many girls, even to this day, are reared to believe in a fairy-tale progression of life—namely, from school to marriage to family to living happily ever after. The fact is that for the modern woman life includes school, work and/or marriage and family (which often includes continuing to work out of choice or necessity) and return to work when the youngest child enters school. The fact is too that the number of those who "live happily ever after" is diminishing and that divorce and separation are on the increase; thus, a rising number of women are heads of households and work to support these households. Homemaking today is neither a full-time nor a lifetime occupation.

Women have long been conditioned to think that they should not aspire to higher career goals and that they should serve on lower rungs of the occupational ladder than men. It is sexist discrimination that has encouraged this kind of thinking and discouraged many women from entering the occupations of their choice.

NONTRADITIONAL CAREERS FOR WOMEN

Today's woman, in fact, has many options open to her. She need not permit society to pressure her into an early—and, unfortunately, all too often, unhappy—marriage. Instead, she can choose to receive a suitable education leading to a self-fulfilling career accompanied, if she wishes, by a marriage based on mature love.

It is a fable that certain occupations are for males only or, similarly, that certain other occupations are for females only (sexist discrimination of either kind is improper). With very rare exceptions, occupations are sexless. It is not the nature of the work, but tradition and discrimination, that have caused certain occupations to be labeled "male-only." Women can be just as competent as men as dentists, architects, lawyers, physicians, newscasters, carpenters, scientists, engineers, electricians, pharmacists and hundreds of other occupations in which discriminatory practices have kept their percentages very low.

Now and New

Now you need not limit your thinking to the traditional women's occupations. Many changes have taken place in the lives of today's women. With these changes have come unusual challenges and opportunities for career choices—a bonanza of nontraditional careers for women. Barriers are being broken, and the future for the women of America looks brighter with each passing day.

You may have read in the papers that a woman was hired to work as a steeplejack, another as a snow shoveler, a third as a baseball umpire, a fourth as a jockey, a fifth as a doorwoman and on and on into many occupations where these women are the first of their sex to hold these positions. These are significant of the changes that are taking place, but even more important to you is what is happening in the broad range of nontraditional occupations in the big, wide world of work.

Since the vast majority of women have been confined to working in a limited number of fields, the number of nontraditional occupations for women is large. Discrimination against women in the working world has been extensive. In some fields, discrimination has been so rampant that little information is available on the small number of women workers in those fields. Consequently, information and figures that this writer obtained from various sources about some of these fields were sometimes contradictory; this writer made every possible effort to trace them down to the most reliable source.

This book covers more than 500 nontraditional occupations which will in the remaining years of this decade collectively offer women millions of employment opportunities. There are many additional nontraditional occupations which will in the future be opening their doors to women, but I have attempted in this book to cover those major areas which have the potential for offering women the largest number of employment opportunities and/or the greatest gratification and challenge, for these are truly where the action is.

Where the Action Is
The action is in the ten large occupational categories covered in this book—namely, the legal field, medical field, healing arts, the helping professions, math and science, engineering, creative fields, business administration, skilled trades and government services.

This is a unique career book because of the very nature of the subject matter; it is the first and only book on the nontraditional, new and expanding employment opportunities for women. I have made every effort to include as much as possible of the information about each occupation as I deemed necessary.

Wherever possible, I have presented the history of women in the occupation, number of women, nature of the work, qualifications and preparation necessary or desirable for entry into the occupation, entrance and advancement, places of employment, advantages and disadvantages, supply and demand of workers in this occupation, future outlook for women, professional associations and/or unions and sources of further information. Because of the extensive, long-standing discrimination against women in the working world, all of this information could not be obtained and is not available for each of the occupations included in this book.

Salaries have not been included because they are changeable and often vary with geographic location and other factors. Federal legislation now requires that women holding the same positions as men must receive equal pay with men. The salaries received by women in all of the occupations discussed herein should be able to provide them with a varying amount of luxuries above and beyond life's basic necessities, depending, of course, upon the individual personal and family obligations of each woman.

In discussing many of the professional occupations, various degrees have been mentioned and it would probably be well to explain them here.

Institutions of higher education may offer two-year or four-or-more-year educational programs of study (curricula) beyond the high school level. The two-year institutions (junior and community colleges and technical institutes) confer the associate degree, the A.A. (associate in arts) or A.S. (associate in science) degree, upon their graduates. The four-year colleges award the bachelor's degree to those who successfully complete four-year undergraduate programs; the popularly conferred bachelor's degrees are the B.A. (bachelor of arts) and B.S. (bachelor of science).

More than four years of post–secondary school study are generally required for entry into the professions. The master's degree (M.A., master of arts, or M.S., master of science) is conferred upon the successful completion of a prescribed one- or two-year program of study on the graduate school level of a university.

Doctoral degrees are conferred upon those who successfully

complete all of the advanced graduate studies and other requirements in specialized professional programs. There are a number of recognized doctorates and the most popular of them are the D.D.S. (doctor of dental surgery), D.V.M. (doctor of veterinary medicine), Ed.D. (doctor of education), J.D. (juris doctor, a fairly new degree which has replaced the L.L.B., bachelor of laws and letters, previously conferred upon law school graduates), M.D. (doctor of medicine) and Ph.D. (doctor of philosophy).

There are so many nontraditional occupations to discuss and so much to say about each that this book could very well have become encyclopedic in size. This could also have occurred if I had given each occupation as much space as the members of that occupation might like. I did not want this book to be encyclopedic and cumbersome. I wanted it to be readable and useful and, therefore, have had to be quite concise about a number of occupations; often the number of potential employment opportunities in an occupation helped to determine how much space would be allotted to that occupation. However, I have attempted never to sacrifice basic, fundamental information of value to the reader for the sake of conciseness.

All right, now, let us look in on the nontraditional occupations for women. Success and fulfillment await the intelligent, ambitious woman who has the abilities, interests and intestinal fortitude needed to break into a field dominated by men.

Since we seek justice for women, let us start our examination of the new and expanding opportunities for women with the field which involves justice—namely, the legal field.

Chapter 2

PORTIAS
IN THE LEGAL FIELD

YOU may have read Shakespeare's *Merchant of Venice*. If you have, you know that, in one of the scenes, the heroine, Portia, disguises herself as a lawyer. "Portia" has, as a result, come to mean a woman lawyer.

Arabella Babb Mansfield was the first American Portia to be admitted to a state bar. "To be admitted to the state bar" means to be permitted to practice law, to serve as a lawyer, within a particular state. Arabella Mansfield's notable achievement took place on June 15, 1869, in Mount Pleasant, Iowa.

The first law school in the United States to admit women was St. Louis Law School, which is now Washington University Law School, in St. Louis, Missouri. This too took place in 1869, and two women were admitted. In 1885, a female became a student at Yale Law School for the first time. She entered surreptitiously before the admissions officers discovered they had accepted a woman. Resisting the pressure put upon her by the professors and male students, she remained and ultimately received her law degree.

Some years ago, Clarence Darrow, the noted attorney, said to a meeting of women lawyers: "You can't be shining lights at the bar because you are too kind. You can never be corporation lawyers because you are not cold-blooded. You have not a high grade of intellect. You can never expect to get the fees men get. I doubt if you even make a living."

Women lawyers have been proving how wrong the eminent Mr. Darrow was when he said this. However, although more than a hundred years have passed since Arabella Mansfield was admitted to the bar, women lawyers continue to contend with the biases shown toward them by their male colleagues.

Prejudices against women in the legal profession and barriers to their admission to law schools have been so strong that in the middle of the twentieth century, there were only some 5,000 female lawyers. Even today, there are male lawyers who believe that law is solely a man's profession and that women do not belong in it. Those who feel this way now, however, are tending to lower their voices when they express their prejudiced views.

Although the male members of the legal profession have never been too eager to welcome women into their ranks, the doors have been opening. It is true that they have been opening very slowly, but now you can push the portals wide open to the appealing opportunities which, for many years, have been available only to men.

There are some heartening signs and chief among them are these encouraging figures. In 1955, there were approximately 241,000 lawyers in this country, of whom about 5,000 were females. Thus, women represented 2.1 per cent of the total number of lawyers in the United States at that time. In 1970, there were 355,242 lawyers in the United States, and 9,103 (2.8 per cent) of them were women. The number of female lawyers almost doubled in this fifteen-year period; the percentage rise may be small, but it is significant and shows that positive changes have been taking place. Even more important is the fact that the number of women entering law schools quadrupled from 1966 to 1971. In 1972, there were more than 10,000 women lawyers, representing about 3 per cent of the total number.

Lawyers are also known as *attorneys* and *counselors at law.*

The people who come to them for legal help are known as their clients. Attorneys make available to their clients a wide variety of legal assistance; they offer them services and advice regarding their legal rights and obligations and may, if necessary, represent them in court. Lawyers handle criminal and civil lawsuits. They spend many hours gathering together evidence to defend their clients; a good deal of time is spent in research and writing up information needed to start and successfully conduct and conclude a legal action.

Lawyers may argue cases before judges and juries, and they may also negotiate settlements out of court. There are lawyers who spend a great deal of time trying cases in court, whereas others may rarely, and perhaps even never, appear in court. Lawyers also devote much time to the preparation of a wide variety of legal documents, such as miscellaneous contracts, wills and trusts. They may serve as executors, guardians and trustees.

Much of what lawyers do depends upon where and for whom they work and the kind of practice they have. Most male—and some female—lawyers have a general private practice, which means they work for themselves or in partnership or association with other lawyers and handle all types of legal matters, both civil and criminal, for their clients.

Some lawyers specialize and limit their practice to a particular aspect of the law. There are *criminal lawyers* and *civil lawyers*. The criminal lawyers handle cases involving offenses against society or the government, such as theft, arson and murder. The title "civil lawyer" is applied to those attorneys who practice exclusively in branches of law other than criminal. Among the civil lawyers are those who specialize in such areas as corporation, divorce, labor, negligence, patent, probate and real estate law.

The *corporation lawyers* act as the legal agents of their corporation-employers in all types of legal transactions involving their employers. They often advise the corporations in matters regarding their legal obligations, privileges and rights. Corporations have been reluctant to hire women attorneys, and the number of female corporation lawyers is small.

The *divorce lawyers* specialize in legal matters involved in annulment, separation and divorce proceedings. Before initiating divorce actions, they may attempt to bring about a reconciliation. Women attorneys feel quite at home in the domestic relations field; their sensitivity to the needs of children makes them gravitate especially to child custody cases.

The *labor lawyers* may work for labor unions or industrial organizations and handle all legal matters pertaining to strikes, wage-hour disputes and other employee-employer relations problems. A limited number of women serve as labor lawyers.

The *negligence lawyers* handle cases involving accidents and other matters where there has been negligence. They may go to court or may negotiate for and obtain a satisfactory settlement out of court. Here, too, the number of female lawyers is limited.

The *patent lawyers* are specialists in patent law. They give advice to inventors, manufacturers and similar clients in regard to the patentability of their inventions. They prepare the patent applications and present them to the U.S. Patent Office. This is a specialty in which women have rarely been found.

The *probate lawyers* plan and settle estates. They prepare wills, deeds of trusts and all other documents pertinent to their clients' estates. Some women attorneys find this specialty appealing, particularly where it involves the protection of children and widows and the guardianship of children.

The *real estate lawyers* are specialists in legal matters involving the sale and transfer of real property. They prepare such documents as deeds, leases and mortgages. Very few female lawyers limit their legal practices solely to this specialty.

Young people who aspire to legal careers should have a deep desire to see justice rendered. They should enjoy working with people and have the ability to gain the confidence of those with whom they work. To succeed in the legal profession, female as well as male prospective attorneys should be above average in intelligence, mentally alert and very self-confident.

Lawyers need exceptional reasoning ability to understand and logically analyze problems in order to be of best possible assistance to their clients. They should be tactful and show good judgment and a sense of discretion. Lawyers should be able to express themselves well. They should have the ability to write, since they are called upon to prepare miscellaneous briefs and documents.

Interestingly, certain qualities which are desirable in male lawyers are often considered undesirable in female lawyers. Law is a field in which the practitioner is expected to have aggression, ambition and drive. Aggressiveness and a combative nature are attributes which help a lawyer to succeed in many of his daily encounters and negotiations.

If a man is aggressive, he is viewed positively; in a woman, this same characteristic often is considered a negative feature. However, not all of a lawyer's work activities call for a combative personality. On the contrary, many legal situations, such as domestic and family relations, require the gentleness and emotional qualities often attributed to women. Most important of all, it must be remembered that no attributes are the exclusive property of either sex. There are men who are gentle and not at all aggressive, and there are women who are very aggressive and not very gentle. Additionally, the same individual, female or male, may at different times, as each situation requires, exhibit contrasting characteristics.

To become a member of the legal profession, a young person generally needs seven years of college and law school study after high school graduation. Preferably, prospective lawyers should complete four years of college and receive the undergraduate college degree (usually the B.A., bachelor of arts), although there are some law schools which accept students who have completed only three years of college study. While at college, they should strive for good marks and arrange to take the Law School Admission Test to gain admission to an approved law school.

After successful completion of three years of full-time study (or four years of part-time, evening session study) at law school, the graduate receives the bachelor of laws and letters (L.L.B.) degree; a number of law schools recently started to confer the juris doctor (J.D.) degree on their graduates.

Women are now accepted into all law schools in the United States, although there are admissions officers in some of the schools who give the female candidates a rather rough time at the admissions interview before accepting them. Even today there are admissions officers who tell female law school candidates that women belong in the kitchen and not in the courtroom.

Many young women find it desirable—and, at times, necessary —to work during the day and attend law school in the evenings.

Before engaging in the practice of law, the law school graduate must pass a written examination given by the state board of bar examiners and be admitted to the state bar. Some neophyte law-yers open their own offices and go into independent practice, but their number is small, since the opportunities for beginners to earn sufficient income in this manner are limited.

Most beginners seek salaried positions and join law firms where they earn and learn by assisting experienced lawyers. Others become law clerks to judges, work as *Legal Aid Society lawyers* or *public defenders,* become members of the legal departments of large organizations or social agencies or enter government employment with either federal, state or local agencies.

Female law school graduates generally find it more difficult to obtain their first positions than do their male colleagues. As a result of Title VII of the Civil Rights Act of 1964 and the state fair employment practices laws, this situation is changing, albeit slowly.

More female beginners than male tend to enter government

employment rather than become associated with a law firm or go into independent practice. In government, they are assured equal pay with their male colleagues. As government attorneys, they may establish law enforcement procedures and argue cases in behalf of the local, state or federal agency for which they work. They may also prepare drafts of legislation, offer advice to government officials and employees regarding laws and regulations and perform a variety of administrative and legal functions. There are burgeoning gratifying opportunities in government service for women attorneys.

NettaBell Girard Larson, the President of the National Association of Women Lawyers, has some noteworthy comments to make about her service as a government attorney.

"I have often been asked why (or how) I decided to go to law school," says Ms. Larson. "I must admit, there is no pat, easy answer; there are many factors which contributed to my final decision. As a grade school child, I can remember my grandmother's comments on the worthwhileness of a legal education and her expression of the hope that I would pursue such an education. In junior high, I was an avid reader of Erle Stanley Gardner and dreamed of becoming a female 'Portia.' My parents were a constant source of encouragement during high school and college as well as in law school."

"The University of Wyoming," continues Ms. Larson, "was, when I attended, a very small law school. I was the only woman student during my junior and senior years. The school had a total enrollment of less than one hundred. There were nine students in my graduating senior class of 1961, the smallest in the history of the school. At twenty-two, I was the youngest practicing lawyer in the state, and remained so for several years."

Ms. Larson adds, "When I finished law school, I started practicing law by myself—a somewhat sort of scary undertaking for a young lawyer. As any lawyer could attest, the first year is like nothing else they have ever experienced. It is difficult, indeed, to jump into the morass of forms, complaints, filing procedures, interrogatories, depositions and trials.

"Not quite four years ago, I had the opportunity to become a 'government lawyer.' The job sounded exciting; in fact, Washington, D.C., sounded exciting, and so I left my home town and my lovely office in Riverton, Wyoming, to broaden my horizons. Within a few months after I started working on the General Counsel's staff for the Department of Housing and Urban Development, I was appointed the first woman (and the youngest lawyer) Section Chief. As Chief of the Section for Interstate Land Sales, I was the Chief Counsel to the Administrator of the Office of Interstate Land Sales Regulation. Approximately 20 per cent of the lawyers on the General Counsel's Staff at HUD were women while I was there. This is, indeed, a large percentage compared to the percentage of women in the legal profession."

"This high percentage," continues Ms. Larson, "indicates the opportunity available for women in government employment. It is an unusual opportunity to gain experience and confidence in a specialized area as well as a unique opportunity to find out what it is like to be a lawyer before jumping into the often confusing arena of private practice. I would highly recommend government experience for either the lawyer who is interested in learning a particular specialty and making a career of it or for the lawyer who wants to become exposed to the area of administrative law for a limited period of time and then expand his or her horizons into other areas. For the young lawyer it can be a unique learning experience because of the contact with more experienced lawyers."

In conclusion, the President of the National Association of Women Lawyers states: "I would recommend a legal career to the woman who likes to work with people and their problems because the lawyer does have a tremendous impact upon individual problems and the solutions thereof. I would further recommend the legal profession to young women who are career

39

oriented and want a lifetime career rather than a spasmodic part-time career when the opportunity arises between child raising and the like."

"I would qualify my statement," she adds, "by saying that there are many successful women lawyers who have families, but few of these have interrupted their careers at any time for more than a few weeks at a time. I would not recommend pursuing a legal education to a woman who does not intend to practice law. Since this is not an a priori or scientific discipline, a woman who wishes to develop her mind through education should seek another less dogmatized field."

In November, 1972, NettaBell Girard Larson returned to the three-room office building which her father had built for her on Main Street in Riverton, Wyoming, to practice law with her husband, also an attorney.

Young lawyers who choose to work for the government may also become attorneys in their city or state corporation counsel's office. The *corporation counsel* is also called the city or state *solicitor.* Increasing numbers of young women attorneys are being hired as *assistant corporation counsels.* They perform a variety of legal activities for the city or state which employs them, including representing their city or state in litigation and offering advice on miscellaneous legal matters.

Government lawyers may advance or be appointed to the post of *attorney-general,* the highest legal officer of the state or federal government. There are a number of women serving as *assistant attorneys-general.*

Some young lawyers are intrigued by the work of the *district attorney* (often referred to as the "D.A.") and, after their graduation from law school, they apply for positions as assistants in their city or county district attorney's office. The number of female *assistant district attorneys* and *district attorneys* is small, but it is growing. More women are being appointed annually to serve as assistant D.A.s and thus more have the opportunity to advance eventually to the post of D.A.

The D.A. is also known as the *prosecutor*. She appears in court against the accused in behalf of the city, county, state or federal government. Before she goes to court, she gathers and analyzes evidence against the accused; she reviews and considers regulations, decisions and other related legal matter.

Large law firms are hiring more women attorneys than ever before. Those young women who succeed in obtaining a salaried position with such firms find that it usually takes much longer for them to become partners in the firm than it does for the male members of the firm; however, the knowledge they generally gain by working with the experienced attorneys is invaluable.

Portias who possess firm social convictions may join community action programs or civic agencies to fight for causes that are of special concern to them. There are expanding opportunities for women lawyers to serve in disadvantaged areas to assist members of minority groups in their fight for their constitutional rights. Young women lawyers with strong consciences are needed to aid the aged, the underprotected and the helpless.

It is rarer and harder for a woman to open her own law office and engage in independent practice than for a man to do so because it is far more difficult for her to build up a clientele sufficient to assure her a suitable annual income. It takes a great deal of courage, ability, hard work and determination to do this. Yet there are women attorneys who have succeeded at it. Lillian D. Rock is such an attorney. A prominent, successful member of the bar of the State of New York, Ms. Rock received her L.L.B. degree from Brooklyn Law School. Upon admission to the bar, she founded her own law firm, now the firm of Rock and Rock, of which she is senior member, with offices at the same address in the Grand Central area of New York City for over twenty-five years.

Ms. Rock was the cofounder of the International Federation of Women Lawyers, which now has branches in every continent of the world. "During my career," she says, "hundreds of women have come to me for advice regarding entry into the legal profession. I have always answered in the affirmative because if a young woman found later she was unsuited she would very likely become a 'drop-out' on her own and never thereafter feel frustrated because, 'but for Lillian Rock, she might have become the Portia of the century.' "

"While the movies encourage many to consider the practice of the law as a full-time career, do not be misled by fiction," advises this noted attorney. "Law deals with facts and reality," she adds, "while the movies deal with fiction and entertainment. In one respect only may the law be likened to a play because both require many weeks and months of preparation before being introduced to the public or in court. Similarly, it may take months to prepare for trial. Ninety per cent of the case is won in your own office and ten per cent in the courts—as you sow so you reap!"

"Processing the details of a case," continues Ms. Rock, "is very tedious, but so is knitting a sweater. It is finished stitch by stitch —dropping a stitch may cause a misfit—or like building a house —brick by brick—the loss of a brick may cause the house to crumble. The trial of a case or its negotiation for settlement requires detailed knowledge of all the facts—without facts, you cannot apply the law or the equity. I have found *no royal road to success*—and no short cut to a successful career. If you follow this discipline, you will find wide expression for your talents."

Ms. Rock states: "My legal profession and my practice of the law have brought me to the participation in the preparation and trial of cases not only in most of the countries of Western Europe but nearly all of the continents of the world. In my own particular case, due to changes in the law following the requirements of the present-day economy, ecology and industrial life,

I have added to my general practice of the law various specialties, such as (but not limited to) the following: the changes required in the making and drafting of wills, administration and management of business, estates, tax procedures, tax exemptions, real estate, insurance, corporation law, domestic relations, as well as changes in the criminal and negligence laws and various other specialties to meet the needs of today."

"But," continues Ms. Rock, "I would advise the future woman lawyer, after receiving a background in the elements of substantive and adjective law, to select the special branch of the law best suited to her talents and to pick herself a little village with a better opportunity to develop a fuller life (most of the great men of history have emanated from small hamlets)—and then let the new woman plant her feet firmly in the soil with her eyes to the heavens and her mind free and imaginative. She will be surprised to find herself exposed to events—which her own instincts and experience will attract—that may someday lead her to a mission in many parts of the world, as it did me."

After several years of practical experience as attorneys, some lawyers who are interested in judicial careers seek to become *judges*. Judges arbitrate and administer justice in courts of law. There are many different types of courts, ranging from local small claims courts and domestic relations courts to the State Supreme Court up to the United States Supreme Court, the highest court in the land.

There are approximately 10,000 judges, ranging from the local *magistrates* to the *Supreme Court Justices,* in all of the courts throughout this country; of this number, fewer than 200 are females. These women are serving as magistrates and judges in courts, small and large, on the municipal through the federal levels. Depending upon the nature and level of the court over which they will preside, judges may be elected to their judgeships or appointed by their mayor, governor or the President of the United States. The day is probably not too far off when a woman will be appointed by the President of the United States to serve as a Justice of the United States Supreme Court.

The future for women in the legal profession looks extremely bright. The increased need for and use of legal services by members of low- and middle-income groups and the anticipated expansion of business will result in a demand for more attorneys, and women attorneys will be needed to help meet this demand.

If a man says you do not belong in the legal profession, tell him to look at the symbol of justice. Who is it that is holding the balanced scale? The symbol of justice is a female!

The noted Judge Dorothy Kenyon, a pioneer among women lawyers whose legal career exceeded fifty years before she passed away in February, 1972, at the age of eighty-three, stated it precisely some years ago when she said, "There is a growing school of thought, including such an eminent authority as Judge Jerome Frank, that regards the entire field of law as feminine rather than masculine. If the subject matter of law is human relations, the rules of conduct of human beings in society, can it be that law is peculiarly women's field after all—women who are supposed, if nothing else, to be experts in human relations, women who are the lawgivers, the prosecutors, the jury, the judges of their young, mediators of disputes to tax the wisdom of Solomon, diplomats of the first water and, proverbially, speakers of the last word?"

When Dorothy Kenyon was a young girl, she asked her lawyer-father, "Can girls be lawyers, father?"

He replied, simply, "Why not, my dear?"

Yes, why not?

Realistically, it must be admitted that perhaps in no other profession has prejudice against females been as formidable as in law; but, despite this, the barriers are crumbling, and the employment future for women in the legal profession looks ever brighter.

If you would like additional information about legal careers and a list of approved law schools, write to any one or all of the following: National Association of Women Lawyers, 1155 E. 60th St., Chicago, Ill. 60637; American Bar Association, 1155 E. 60th St., Chicago, Ill. 60637; and/or the Association of American Law Schools, 1 DuPont Circle N.W., Washington, D.C. 20036.

It has become apparent in recent years that the number of lawyers is insufficient to meet the increasing demands for legal services. To help ease this situation, a new occupation, the *legal paraprofessional,* has arisen. The job of the *legal assistant,* the legal paraprofessional, is to free the lawyer of routine tasks and thus enable her lawyer-employer to have more time to provide professional legal services to more clients. There will be need for many thousands of legal assistants throughout the 1970s, and the employment future is indeed bright for those who obtain approved training in this paraprofession.

The occupation of the legal assistant is described in detail in this writer's *Paraprofessions: Careers of the Future and the Present* (Julian Messner, 1972). You can also obtain additional information by writing to the American Bar Association, Special Committee on Legal Assistants, 1155 E. 60th St., Chicago, Ill. 60637.

Chapter 3

FEMALE PHYSICIANS AND SURGEONS

HAVE you or any member of your family visited a medical doctor recently? Were you annoyed because his attitude toward you was impersonal and, perhaps, indifferent, distant and cold? If you were, then you are typical of an increasing number of patients who lodge these complaints against male doctors.

People who are ill are in need of thoughtfulness, consideration, tenderness and empathy. These qualities are generally considered feminine. Actually, they are neither masculine nor feminine; they are traits which all human beings should possess. Unfortunately, whereas females feel free to express their emotions, males, in our society, are often taught to repress theirs.

The medical profession needs more women *medical doctors* (also called *physicians*) not only to help meet the dire shortage of physicians and the growing demands for medical services, but also to bring the qualities of kindness, compassion and empathy to the ill and the injured.

People no longer laugh when a young woman says she would like to embark on a medical career, as they did in the days of Elizabeth Blackwell. When she decided to become a physician, it took tremendous persistence and boldness to break through the barriers against the entry of a female into a medical school. It took great courage for Elizabeth Blackwell to withstand the

ing and earning experience. *Interns* learn by working
he supervision of experienced physicians and earn a salary
ie hospitals in which they serve. After completing this
iip, the young physicians may open their own medical
and become *general practitioners* (*G.P.s*).

new medical doctors, however, are not becoming gen-
ictitioners. The general practitioner has a medical practice
h the physician has patients of all ages and treats illnesses
uries of all kinds. So much new medical information has
ccumulated in the past twenty-five years that many young
ans decide to specialize in one particular branch of the
l field. Therefore, after completing their internship, they
.e on in a hospital for a further two- to five-year period
inced training known as a "residency." The doctors in a
cy are called *"resident physicians"* or *"residents."*

exact length of residency for each hospital resident de-
upon the branch of medicine in which the resident is
zing. Residents supervise the interns in their service. The
ts, in turn, work under the supervision of the hospital's
ng physicians. The medical profession has, in recent years,
ffering its women physicians the opportunity to combine
ge, children and career. Thus, there are some residencies,
s in psychiatry, which the physician can complete by
the hospital on a part-time basis.

the residents have completed their hospital residency
g, they may open their own offices and start a private
e in their specialties. They are not considered certified
l *specialists*, however, until they have passed a specialty
examination and met all the requirements of the specialty
There are almost forty specialties and subspecialties recog-
>y the American Medical Association.

ile physicians differ from male physicians in the special-
y prefer. Approximately 19 per cent of the female medical
are *pediatricians*, which makes pediatrics their most pop-

mockery of those around her. Yet she persisted, and in 1849 she
became the first woman in America to earn a medical degree.

For more than a hundred years, the medical school environment continued to be hostile to women. Medical school admissions officers made it exceedingly difficult for females to be
accepted. Those who were successful in gaining admission all
too often were harassed by professors and students alike. As a
result, in 1970, women constituted only 7 per cent of the medical
profession.

Admittedly, too, the number of female physicians is small
because, for the past several decades, most girls have been reared
to believe that the medical profession, like the legal field, is a
man's domain. Thus, only few female college students dared to
consider medicine as a career. This situation began to change
at the end of the 1960s and the start of the 1970s, stimulated in
great part by the Women's Liberation movement. In the past
few years, increasing numbers of young women have been going
to medical school and entering the medical profession.

At the start of 1972, out of a total of 344,823 physicians in
the United States, there were 27,034 women physicians; this
represented 7.8 per cent of the total number of medical doctors.
In the 1959–60 first-year class in the medical schools throughout
the United States, females represented 6.4 per cent of the total
number of students accepted; in 1971–72, females represented 13
per cent of the total. This is a significant increase and hopefully
indicates that the percentage of women in the medical profession
will continue to rise.

We have a long way to go, however, to equal the percentages
of women physicians in other countries. In 1965, women represented 65 per cent of the total number of medical doctors in the
Soviet Union, 30 per cent in Poland, 25 per cent in the Philip-
pines, 25 per cent in Korea, 20 per cent in West Germany, 20
per cent in Chile, 19 per cent in Italy, 16 per cent in Great
Britain, 16 per cent in Denmark, 13 per cent in Brazil and 12

per cent in India. Even in Japan and Spain, where young women live comparatively more sheltered lives than in the United States, 9 per cent of the physicians were women.

Women are urgently needed to alleviate the dire need for medical doctors in this country. Physicians are needed to treat the ill and the injured, the aged and disabled. Medical doctors not only work hard to cure the patients' sicknesses and to make them well again, but also are concerned with preventive medicine. Annual checkups are an important means of practicing preventive medicine.

Sometimes physicians must do surgery (perform operations) in order to restore the patient's health. Physicians treat patients of all ages. They help not only those who are ill from diseases but also those who have been injured in accidents.

Medicine is a highly appealing profession. Like the legal profession, it carries with it a great deal of prestige. Patients cannot help but look up to the physicians who take away their aches and pains.

Those who would like to discourage women from becoming medical doctors say that women are squeamish and cannot stand the sight of blood or of a needle being injected into the body of a patient. Surely, there are women who get upset at the sight of blood; just as surely, there are also men who faint when they see blood. This trait has absolutely nothing to do with the sex of the individual; it is a myth that some people try to perpetuate to keep women out of the medical profession, and it should go the way of all myths that aim to prevent women from using their God-given talents and intelligence to enter and succeed in their fields of interest. Interestingly, these same people accept the fact that nurses are not squeamish and can stand the sight of blood, but they are content that women should remain as nurses, as a step below the physicians.

If you want to be of service to humanity, if you would like to heal the ill and the injured and to help the aged and disabled,

---

if you are considerate and sympatheti[c]
in intelligence, a superior student a[nd]
especially the biological sciences, med[icine]
you.

To become a physician, you must [get high]
marks in all of the required premedica[l]
the prospective physician must take [the Ad-]
mission Test. Competition for entry i[s]
keen, and candidates for admission [must]
The medical school program leading [to the]
(M.D.) degree takes four years to [complete]
universities that are combining their [undergraduate]
medical school curricula into seven-yea[r and]
six-year programs by adding summer s[essions]
accepted today in all of the medical s[chools]

Unlike the legal field, where it is po[ssible]
by attending late afternoon or eve[ning classes]
schools have only day session program[s]
is costly, but if you are earnest about [it and]
have the necessary ability, you need no[t worry]
There are public medical schools, s[upported by]
funds, where the tuition fees are not v[ery high]
federal government, the medical scho[ols and]
organizations give financial help to d[eserving students]
assist them through their medical trai[ning]
members of other minority groups are [encouraged]
and aided to attend medical school.

At the graduation ceremonies, the [graduates]
take the Oath of Hippocrates, by whi[ch they pledge]
the high traditions of their profession. [From this point]
forward add the initials "M.D." after t[heir names]

The medical school graduate must pa[ss a]
and serve an approved hospital inter[nship]
before being permitted to practice me[dicine]

---

a lea[r]
under[]
from []
inter[n]
offices[]

Mo[]
eral p[]
in wh[]
and i[]
been [a]
physi[c]
medic[]
conti[n]
of ad[]
reside[]

The[]
pend[s]
speci[a]
reside[]
atten[d]
been []
marri[]
such []
servi[]

Af[]
train[i]
pract[]
*medi[*]
boar[d]
boar[d]
nize[d]

Fe[]
ties t[]
doct[]

ular specialty. Among the male doctors, only about 5 per cent are pediatricians. Surgery is the most popular specialty among the men, with about 24 per cent of them serving as *surgeons,* whereas less than 4 per cent of the women are surgeons.

The *pediatrician* limits her practice to work with children. She is concerned about preventing and treating the illnesses and injuries which occur in children, generally, to the age of sixteen.

Surgeons do major operations on patients; often general practitioners do surgery too, but these are usually minor operations. Surgeons operate to remove a tumor, to repair a broken bone (fracture), to prevent disease from spreading throughout the body, to correct a body deformity or for a miscellany of other reasons.

There are some surgeons who limit their practice to surgery on certain areas of the body or special types of operations (such as *orthopedic surgeons*) or on one organ of the body (such as *heart surgeons*). They may specialize further in a subbranch of surgery, such as plastic surgery. *Plastic surgeons* operate to repair damaged or mutilated parts of the body and face and to improve upon the natural appearance of the patient.

Female and male medical doctors share the same second most popular specialty—namely, internal medicine. Fourteen and a half per cent of the female and 18.5 per cent of the male physicians are *internists.*

Do not confuse the title *"internist"* with that of *"intern."* As you learned earlier in this chapter, the *intern* is the young medical doctor, newly graduated from medical school, who is serving an internship in a hospital. The *internist* is a physician, with a number of years of experience, who is a specialist in internal medicine.

The *internist* specializes in diagnosing and treating diseases and disorders of the internal organs. The latter include the heart, lungs, liver, stomach, intestines, kidneys and other organs inside the body cavity. Internists work with adult patients; they start

51

where the pediatricians stop. They are personal physicians to adults. Patients come to them when they believe something is wrong with the insides of their bodies. They also visit their internists for their annual checkups to be sure that no trouble has developed during the year and, if some trouble has arisen, to catch it in its early stages.

There are internists who study further and become especially expert in one particular internal organ. They become specialists in one of the subspecialties of internal medicine. Thus, there are internists who complete a period of advanced training in the subspecialty of cardiology (the study of the heart) and are called *cardiologists* (heart specialists).

Psychiatry is the third most popular specialty among female physicians. About 14 per cent of the female doctors are *psychiatrists,* as compared with 7 per cent of the male doctors. Psychiatrists are concerned with the mental illnesses which plague people. When the family physician or the internist recognizes that a patient's "physical" illness is more mental than physical, the patient may be referred to a psychiatrist. Psychiatrists may listen to their patients as they talk out their troubles, or the psychiatrists may give their patients any one or more of the new chemicals which help in the treatment of mental disorders, or perhaps they may do both.

Among male physicians, general practice is their third most popular type of practice, including 18 per cent of all male physicians. This is the fourth choice among female doctors, including 11 per cent of their number.

General practitioners of recent times have been finding that they must make many changes in their practice to keep pace with their profession. There is so much to know, and so many advances have taken place since medicine entered the space age that the general practitioner today needs additional preparation and training. Like their medical colleagues, the specialists, the general practitioners too have found that they must become specialists. Thus, in 1969, the Advisory Board for Medical Specialties and the Council on Medical Education of the American Medical Association gave official recognition to the new specialty of "family practice."

The G.P. is, therefore, giving way to the *F.P.* (*family physician* or *family practitioner*). The physician who wishes to become an F.P. must complete a hospital residency in family practice and then pass a board examination in this specialty.

F.P.s are concerned about the total health care and needs of their patients. They recognize the effects of each patient's environment on the patient's family. Their awareness of the connections between the mind and the body give them skill in understanding how a person's feelings and mental problems often make that person physically sick. F.P.s not only treat people after they become ill, but also try to prevent them from becoming ill.

The next most popular specialties for women doctors are anesthesiology, pathology and obstetrics/gynecology. *Anesthesiologists* cooperate with the surgeons and supply various forms of anesthetic drugs to patients to prevent these patients from feeling any pain during surgical procedures.

Pathologists are specialists in pathology, the science of disease. They interpret the changes which illnesses have brought about in the body's organs, tissues and cells as well as modifications in body chemistry due to miscellaneous diseases.

Obstetricians limit their practice to the delivery of babies and to the care of mothers before, during and after childbirth. *Gynecologists* also have only female patients, but they limit themselves to diagnosing and treating diseases of the female reproductive organs. Often the obstetrician and the gynecologist are one and the same physician.

Dr. Frances Keller Harding, the Immediate Past President of the American Medical Women's Association, is an obstetrician-gynecologist. Born in Walla Walla, Washington, the only child of Drs. Martin and Florence Keller, Dr. Harding has been active in Columbus, Ohio, for thirty years in private practice and at the Ohio State University.

"My parents were in practice in New Zealand for twenty years, and I lived 'down under' the first thirteen years of my life," says Dr. Harding. "I later practiced medicine in Australia for eight years. During that time, I helped start the first Planned Parenthood Clinic in that country and, on several occasions, I spent time in the Fiji Islands, New Guinea and the Solomon Islands traveling in thirty-five- to forty-eight-foot auxiliary ketches which served as medical facilities."

"My choice of obstetrics and gynecology as a special field," explains Dr. Harding, "was encouraged by my father's interest in obstetrics and my mother's specialty of obstetrics and gynecology, which she practiced actively for sixty-five years. Having grown up in an environment of active medical service, I studied medicine and obtained my M.D. degree from Loma Linda University in California. I received further training at Hollywood Presbyterian Hospital, followed by postgraduate work at Edinburgh University which completed my formal training."

This busy physician is married to Dr. Warren G. Harding II, a surgeon. She says, "We have three children, a daughter in pediatrics, another daughter a dentist and a son who is qualified as a lawyer and a physician. Eight grandchildren aid me in maintaining contact with the younger generation."

Dr. Frances, as she is affectionately called by her patients, says, "I gave up maternity work after twenty years, but still find great enjoyment in following the careers of my 'babies.' My more recent practice has been in the area of gynecological problems of college girls where my understanding and insight have brought great satisfaction with the guidance given to those passing through this trying age."

This remarkable physician has participated in many public services, including serving as President of the Metropolitan Health Council of Columbus, Ohio, and President of Zonta. "My service on many committees and my writing and teaching in the field of family life and medical education for women," she says, "have permitted me to aid in molding the status of problems which are of interest to me. For women doctors of the future, I see a brighter field of acceptance than I experienced."

Dr. Harding offers this advice to these future female physicians: "If marriage and children are in your future, be certain your husbands are supportive to your activities, remain at your feminine best, do your fair share of work in all your pursuits and maintain your dedication of service to the sick."

Smaller numbers of women specialists are *dermatologists,* who diagnose and treat skin diseases; *neurologists,* who diagnose and treat disorders and diseases of the brain, spinal cord and other parts of the nervous system; *ophthalmologists,* who treat diseases and defects of the eyes; *otolaryngologists,* who limit their practice to diseases and disorders of the ear, nose and throat; and *radiologists,* who diagnose and treat diseases by using radium, x-rays and other radioactive substances.

There are women physicians in every specialty, albeit in very small numbers in some of the specialties. Thus, for example, in 1972 there were only forty-three *plastic surgeons* and six *aerospace medicine specialists* among the women physicians. If you decide to enter the medical profession, you may choose to enter one of the specialties in which women have been concentrating; but bear in mind that opportunities are available to you now in all of the specialties. Select the specialty which is of greatest interest to you and for which you have the necessary talent, and then go forth with courage to aim for and enter into it.

The majority of women physicians have their own private practices. Most of the remainder work in hospitals, clinics, health centers, state and local health departments, medical schools, private industry and research foundations. Of those in private practice, most are in practice by themselves.

NONTRADITIONAL CAREERS FOR WOMEN

There is a growing trend now toward sharing one's practice with another physician or going into group practice. Group practice makes life easier for the physician; for the woman physician, it makes it more possible for her to combine a medical career with home and family responsibilities. Group practice will enable you to have a more regular professional schedule, with prearranged days off and vacation periods. Sharing a medical practice is much less wearing on each physician than carrying the patient load alone.

Physicians are also tending to work in closer contact with their communities. Community health centers are opening up throughout the country to provide health care to people within their own neighborhoods.

Medicine is an expanding, exciting field, and there is adventure in it for all who enter. There is much work to be done to learn how to cure—and, better yet, to prevent—such illnesses as asthma, cancer, cystic fibrosis, diabetes, epilepsy, glaucoma, heart disease, kidney disease, lung disorders, mental illnesses, multiple sclerosis and muscular dystrophy.

To physicians comes the great satisfaction of knowing that they are helping their fellow human beings to get well and/or to stay well. Medical doctors cannot always make the sick well again, nor can they always save the lives of the very ill. However, they do succeed in saving countless numbers of lives, easing their patients' pain and restoring their patients' general good health.

There is a great need for physicians to care for the ill and the injured, the aged and disabled, the infants and the ailing of all ages. As time goes on, more and more medical doctors will be needed. There is urgent need and room for capable, compassionate women of all races and religions in the medical profession.

Paintings have always portrayed the physician as a father figure. Medicine now needs the mother figure, the female physician with her feminine feelings. If you are dedicated and intelligent and have stamina, good emotional and physical health and

56

feeling for your fellow human beings, then enter this profession and do your part to alleviate so much of the suffering in this world.

If you would like to obtain a list of the names and addresses of approved medical schools, as well as further information about careers in medicine, write to one or more of the following: American Medical Women's Association, 1740 Broadway, New York, N.Y. 10019; American Medical Association, 535 N. Dearborn St., Chicago, Ill. 60610; and/or the Association of American Medical Colleges, 1 DuPont Circle N.W., Washington, D.C. 20036.

Like the legal profession, the medical profession became aware in recent years that there are insufficient members of their profession to meet the growing demands for professional services. A new medical career has, therefore, developed—the *medical paraprofessional*. The medical paraprofessional is called a *physician's assistant*. The physician's assistant works under the direction and supervision of a medical doctor and, by performing numerous subprofessional tasks, enables the physician to serve many more patients. There is tremendous demand and need for the services of physician's assistants, and women who are trained in this paraprofession should have a very bright employment future.

The occupation of the physician's assistant is described in detail in this writer's book on paraprofessions mentioned in the preceding chapter. Additional information can also be obtained by writing to the American Medical Association, Department of Health Manpower, 535 N. Dearborn St., Chicago, Ill. 60610.

Chapter 4

THE HEALING ARTS

MEDICAL doctors constitute only one group, albeit a major one, of the various practitioners in the healing arts who work together to form the health team. Employment in the healing arts has increased tremendously during the past several years. In 1970, these health service occupations together included more than 3,500,000 workers.

Some of these occupations are traditional for women; others are not. Nursing is the largest health occupation and the most traditional for women. In 1972, there were about 748,000 registered nurses and 1,200,000 practical nurses and auxiliary nursing workers; employment opportunities in nursing for the years ahead are excellent.

Since nursing is traditionally a woman's field, and since this book is concerned with nontraditional fields for women, we will not go into any further detail about it here. If you wish further information about registered nurses or licensed practical nurses, write either to the Committee on Nursing Careers, American Nurses Association, 2420 Pershing Road, Kansas City, Mo. 64108, or to the National Federation of Licensed Practical Nurses, 250 West 59th St., New York, N.Y. 10019.

Another large group of doctors in the health service fields, in addition to the medical doctors, is that of the doctors of dental surgery, the *dentists*. They diagnose and treat malformations, diseases and injuries of teeth, gums and other areas in the mouth. In 1972, there were about 103,000 dentists in the United States. Somewhat more than 90 per cent of them were self-employed and had a general "chairside" practice. About 9 per cent of them were specialists. About half of these specialists were *orthodontists*, specialists in the straightening of malpositioned teeth. The remainder were *exodontists*, who specialize in extracting teeth, *pedodontists*, who treat children only, *periodontists*, who specialize in diagnosing and treating diseases and disorders of the gums, and *prosthodontists*, who specialize in work with artificial teeth or dentures.

There is an extremely small number of women dentists. They represent only a bit more than 1 per cent of the dental profession. In 1972, there were about 1,200 women in this profession.

Although a college degree is desirable, a minimum of two years of college, including the completion of the predental courses, is required for admission to dental school. The professional programs in the dental schools are four years in length and, upon the successful completion of these programs, the graduates are awarded the doctor of dental surgery (D.D.S.) or the doctor of dental medicine (D.M.D.) degree. Graduates must pass a board examination and obtain a license before they can practice dentistry.

There are not enough dentists to meet the demands for dental services, and all indications point to an increase in this demand in the years ahead. Excellent opportunities await women who enter this profession. To those who enter come also prestige, very good earning potential and the gratification of knowing that they are helping to keep their patients dentally healthy.

Do you have above-average manual talents, including finger dexterity? If you have these abilities, plus an interest in dental health and scientific studies, superior judgment of space and shape and above average intelligence, you should give serious consideration to a career in dentistry.

NONTRADITIONAL CAREERS FOR WOMEN

Women are urgently needed as dentists throughout the United States. In the Soviet Union, women represent about 83 per cent of the total number of dentists; in Greece, 50 per cent; and in Denmark, France, Norway and Sweden, 23 to 30 per cent.

Here is a superb opportunity for you to enter a field where you can help to meet the rising demands for dental services and work the hours which are most convenient to you. You can combine a dental career with marriage and children by establishing your dental practice within your own home.

To obtain further information and a list of the approved schools of dentistry, write to the American Dental Association, 211 E. Chicago Ave., Chicago, Ill. 60611.

When dentists find that their patients need dentures (artificial teeth), bridges, crowns or any other dental or orthodontic appliances, they take the necessary impressions of their patients' mouths and send these impressions to *dental laboratory technicians,* also known as *dental technicians.*

About 20 per cent of the estimated 34,000 *dental laboratory technicians* in 1972 were women; in a survey taken five years earlier, it was found that only 12 per cent were women. There is little, if any, discrimination against women in this field. Women are becoming aware of the attractiveness of this field, and thus their numbers are rising.

Dental technicians do not see the patients for whom they are making the dentures or other appliances. They are guided by the dentists' impressions and instructions. Some technicians entered this occupation by receiving on-the-job training in a dental laboratory after their high school graduation; this type of apprenticeship generally takes from three to four years to complete. Others entered via a two-year dental laboratory technology program in a junior or community college.

Beginner dental technicians perform rather simple jobs, such as pouring plaster into molds. As they become more experienced and more skilled, they perform more difficult tasks and may specialize in one particular type of dental appliance.

This occupation offers excellent opportunities for women. Physical strength is not required; dental technicians are seated during most (and often all) of their working hours. These technicians need finger dexterity, manual aptitude, good color perception and the ability to follow instructions carefully and do detailed work. Many women possess these qualifications. Those women who wish to work on a part-time basis will find that if they are trained dental technicians, they should have no difficulty finding such part-time employment in dental laboratories.

The employment outlook for dental technicians is very good. After acquiring a good deal of experience and getting to know the dentists in the community, some technicians open dental laboratories of their own. For additional information about careers in dental technology, write to the National Association of Dental Laboratories, Inc., 3801 Mt. Vernon Ave., Alexandria, Va. 22305.

Dental hygienists instruct individuals and groups in the techniques of teeth and mouth care. Under the supervision of a dentist, they clean the patient's teeth, removing deposits, accretions and stains. *Dental assistants* perform a variety of dental office duties to facilitate the work of the dentist as she examines and treats her patients.

There were about 16,000 dental hygienists and 91,000 dental assistants at work in the United States in 1970. Almost all of them were women. Dental hygiene and dental assisting are traditionally women's fields. If you would like additional career information about either or both of these fields, write to the American Dental Hygienists Association, 211 E. Chicago Ave., Chicago, Ill. 60611, and/or the American Dental Assistants Association at the same address.

In addition to the medical doctors, others who employ the

title "physician" are the *osteopathic physicians*. In 1972, there were approximately 13,000 osteopathic physicians, also known as *osteopaths;* about 1,000 of them (about 8 per cent) were women. Almost all of them have private practices, and most serve as general practitioners. They differ essentially from the medical doctors in the stress they place on manipulative therapy and in the special emphasis they give to impairments in the musculoskeletal system.

At least three years of college are required for admission to an approved school of osteopathy. These schools have a four-year program of professional studies leading to the doctor of osteopathy (D.O.) degree. Women are accepted into these schools on an equal basis with men. Like the medical doctors, the osteopaths must pass a licensing examination and internship before they are permitted to practice.

A keen sense of touch, in addition to all the other personal qualifications desirable for physicians, and a belief in the benefits of osteopathic healing techniques and principles are needed by those who would like to become osteopathic physicians. Future trends in this profession appear to be excellent for women, especially in a number of the Midwestern states and Pennsylvania, where this method of healing is widely accepted.

For a list of approved schools of osteopathy and further career information, write to the American Osteopathic Association, 212 E. Ohio St., Chicago, Ill. 60611.

For many years, until quite recent times, veterinary medicine was considered to be a field solely for men. But prejudice against women in this field has begun to diminish. In 1972, there were approximately 800 women *veterinarians* out of a total of approximately 27,500 veterinarians in the United States. Thus, women represented about 3 per cent of all of the doctors of veterinary medicine.

Veterinarians diagnose and treat diseases, disorders and injuries of animals, large and small. They play a vital role in helping to prevent the outbreak and spread of diseases among animals. This is extremely important, for many of these diseases may be transmitted to human beings. Veterinarians help to ensure that our country's supply of food of animal origin is wholesome and disease free. The many functions of veterinarians make them vital members of the public health team.

Most veterinarians are in private practice and are general practitioners treating all sorts and sizes of animals. Some specialize in the illnesses of small pets; others limit their practice to cattle, horses, poultry, sheep or swine. A few thousand veterinarians work for government agencies performing inspection, research and public health functions.

Although the majority of women veterinarians specialize in small animals or pets, they are found in all the areas of veterinary medicine where male veterinarians work, such as large animal practice, meat inspection, research, teaching and work in zoological parks and the military services.

A minimum of two years of college, including the necessary preveterinary courses, is required for admission to any one of the eighteen colleges of veterinary medicine in the United States. The programs in these schools are four years in length and lead to the degree of doctor of veterinary medicine (D.V.M. or V.M.D.). The graduates must pass the examination given by the state board of veterinary examiners and receive the state license before they are permitted to practice.

The number of women entering colleges of veterinary medicine is increasing annually. In 1972, women students represented 11 per cent of the total enrollment at these colleges. When you compare this figure with the fact that in 1972 only 3 per cent of all the veterinarians were women, it is obvious that the number of women doctors of veterinary medicine is soaring upward.

Do you have a pet? Do you like cats and dogs and other domestic animals? Are you concerned about the health of animals? Do you have the physical strength, ability and courage to skillfully handle sick or injured animals? If your replies are "Yes," you should seriously consider a career in veterinary medicine.

Some years ago, people who were not very knowledgeable about the nature of the work of doctors of veterinary medicine called them "horse doctors," rather than veterinarians or the abbreviated term "vets." Those who wished to discourage girls from entering this field found it easy to do so by telling girls they did not have the strength to handle sick horses. Don't let anyone discourage you with this ancient myth. Only a small percentage of veterinarians work with horses, and most women veterinarians work with small animals.

There is a shortage of veterinarians, and the future looks bright indeed for women in this profession. There are also many opportunities for part-time employment, making it easier for those who wish to combine career, home and family responsibilities.

For further information and the names and addresses of the professional schools of veterinary medicine, write to the American Veterinary Medical Association, 600 S. Michigan Ave., Chicago, Ill. 60605.

Women in this profession have an association of their own, the Women's Veterinary Medical Association. Dr. Bonnie V. Gustafson, the President of the W.V.M.A., received her bachelor of science (B.S.) and doctor of veterinary medicine (D.V.M.) degrees from the University of Minnesota.

Says Dr. Gustafson, "I thank my lucky stars for parents who not only wanted me to have a college education at all costs, but who also wanted me to pursue my educational goal, whatever it might be. There was a time when prejudice against women in veterinary medicine was deep-rooted, but I was every bit as prejudiced that women do well as veterinarians. Gratification comes in many forms to a veterinarian. What is more touching than watching a child hug the dog who only days before was so close to death, or seeing the tears in the eyes of an elderly couple whose constant companion was given a few more years to live when a tumor was removed. Interest by variety certainly is gratification—for example, working with an elephant, lion or ostrich."

"Most certainly," continues Dr. Gustafson, "I would recommend a career as a veterinarian for young ladies, and I think the strongest evidence of this is the fact that I am on the faculty at one of our colleges of veterinary medicine. To those who might be interested in choosing my profession as a career, might I suggest that you study your courses like your future depended on them; it does, and don't close your mind to any aspect of the profession because until you know all the different areas open to you, you can not truly benefit from its diversity."

Dr. Gustafson adds: "Today the veterinary profession is no longer limited to the traditional general practice, making it even more attractive to women. Small animal practice, public health, research, consulting and the military are a few of the diversities providing women graduates with a career. Many women veterinarians are satisfactorily combining a family life with their practices, another enigma which no longer applies."

Dr. Gustafson became Dr. Bonnie Gustafson Beaver in November, 1972, showing her faith in the fact that marriage and a veterinary career go well together.

If you would like to obtain more information about the W.V.M.A., write to Dr. Bonnie V. Gustafson, President, Women's Veterinary Medical Association, Texas A & M University, College of Veterinary Medicine, Department of Veterinary Anatomy, College Station, Tex. 77843.

There were about 16,000 *chiropractors* in the United States in 1972. Eight per cent of them, about 1,300, were women. Chiropractors employ manual manipulation of the body, particularly the spinal column, as their basic method of healing. The principle of chiropractic as a system of treatment is that the health of an individual is determined essentially by his nervous system.

Chiropractors believe that anything which interferes with the

65

nervous system hinders the normal functioning of the person's body. They therefore manipulate the spine and any other involved areas which, according to their diagnosis, may be impairing the patient's health. They do not use drugs or surgery, but may employ such supplementary measures as diet, exercise, light, rest, water and heat therapy.

The qualifications for entry into the chiropractic field vary from state to state. Most states require one or two years of preparatory college studies, followed by the successful completion of a four-year program of studies at an approved chiropractic college, leading to the doctor of chiropractic (D.C.) degree. In most states, graduates must pass a state board examination and receive a license before they are permitted to practice chiropractic.

Most graduates go into private practice. Opportunities for women chiropractors appear to be bright, since many who seek this system of healing may prefer to be treated by women. Newly licensed graduates would do best in those sections of the country where chiropractic is a readily accepted method of treatment.

A list of approved chiropractic colleges and further career information may be obtained from the American Chiropractic Association, 2200 Grand Ave., Des Moines, Iowa 50312. The A.C.A. also has a Council of Women Chiropractors; for further information, write to Dr. Madolyn F. Putnam, President, American Council of Women Chiropractors, 22 S. Main St., Bristol, N.H. 03222.

There were about 18,000 *optometrists* practicing in the United States in 1972. A mere 2.8 per cent of them, about 520, were women.

Optometrists are concerned about improving and protecting their patients' vision. They examine the patient's eyes for defects in vision, perform various tests to determine whether visual problems exist, suggest corrective eye exercises and, when necessary, prescribe lenses to correct refractive errors of the eyes. They may prescribe regular and contact lenses, telescopic and micro-scopic lenses or other high-magnification aids.

Optometrists are not permitted to resort to drugs or perform surgery, as ophthalmologists do. If during the process of examin-ing a patient's eyes, the optometrist discovers the presence of a disease or other abnormal condition of the eye calling for medi-cal or surgical treatment, the optometrist then refers the patient to an ophthalmologist.

Many people often confuse the optometrist with the ophthal-mologist and optician. In contrast to the optometrist, the oph-thalmologist is a medical doctor who is a specialist in diseases and disorders of the eyes; also known as an oculist, he is con-cerned with the medical and surgical care of the eyes and, when necessary, prescribes lenses. The optician makes and fits eye-glasses on the basis of prescriptions he has received from optom-etrists and ophthalmologists.

To enter the field of optometry, the student must complete at least two years of college, including preoptometry courses, fol-lowed by the successful completion of four years of training at an accredited school of optometry. There is little, if any, dis-crimination against the admission of female students into these schools. Graduates of these schools are awarded the doctor of optometry (O.D.) degree. They must then pass the required board examination and be licensed to practice optometry.

Most optometrists are self-employed. Most also are in solo practices, but increasing numbers are starting to form partner-ships and group practices. Optometry offers women excellent opportunities for flexible work schedules. The female optometrist, whether in solo, partnership or group practice, can arrange her own hours of work as she may desire or as responsibilities at home may require; for those who may wish it, there are favorable opportunities for part-time practice.

Many children do not do well in school because of reading

problems caused by visual defects. Women who enjoy working with children can obtain tremendous gratification helping these children to see better. Many young people living in the disadvantaged areas of the cities have problems with their vision. There is a shortage of optometrists, and women optometrists, particularly members of minority groups, are urgently needed in these urban areas.

The demand for optometric services far exceeds the supply of optometrists. Women who have the manual dexterity and mechanical aptitude needed to use precision optical instruments, who are interested in scientific studies and health care and who enjoy being of service to people can anticipate a bright employment future if they enter upon a career in optometry.

For further information about optometric careers and a list of accredited schools of optometry, write to the American Optometric Association, 7000 Chippewa St., St. Louis, Mo. 63119. The A.O.A. also has a Washington office, which is engaged in conducting a program to recruit women and members of minority groups into the field of optometry and to aid would-be optometrists with loans, scholarships and any other assistance which they may need. For information about this program, write to Aaron G. Donerson, Director, Minority Recruitment, American Optometric Association, Washington Office, 1730 M St. N.W., Washington, D.C. 20036.

Under the heading *optician,* there are two types of health service personnel. There are the *optical mechanics* (also known as *optical laboratory technicians*) and the *dispensing opticians.*

It was estimated that in 1970 there were about 15,000 optical mechanics and about 11,000 dispensing opticians throughout the United States. It was similarly estimated that approximately 3,000 of the total number of 26,000 opticians were women and that most of these women were dispensing opticians.

Optical mechanics grind and polish lenses according to the specifications on the prescriptions which they have received from

The Healing Arts

ophthalmologists and optometrists. Most optical mechanics do
their work in wholesale optical laboratories; a small number
work for optometrists.

Dispensing opticians fit the prescription glasses directly onto
the customer. They fit lenses in frames, help the customers in
their choice of frames and make the necessary adjustments to
be sure the glasses fit the customer properly. Dispensing opticians
generally work in retail optical stores or optical departments of
department stores; some are employed by ophthalmologists or
optometrists.

Training for careers in optical mechanics or optical dispensing
may be obtained in vocational schools, two-year community college programs in optics, on-the-job training programs or apprenticeship programs, which are four or five years long. Applicants
for these programs should be high school graduates.

Some states require that opticians pass a licensing examination
and be licensed. Check with your state department of education
for the specific requirements of your state.

Women who enjoy and have the ability to do precision work
and who have finger dexterity may be interested in becoming
optical laboratory technicians. Those who like to deal directly
with people and who have a tactful, pleasant personality may
prefer careers as dispensing opticians. The outlook for employment in these occupations is favorable.

Further career information and a list of training programs in
opticianry may be obtained from either the American Board of
Opticianry, 821 Eggert Road, Buffalo, N.Y. 14226, or the Guild
of Prescription Opticians of America, 1250 Connecticut Ave.
N.W., Washington, D.C. 20036.

Pharmacists are essentially specialists in the science of testing,
compounding and dispensing medicines. There were about 13,000
female pharmacists in the United States in 1972; they represented
about 10 per cent of the nearly 130,000 pharmacists practicing
throughout the country. In 1972 too, women pharmacy students

represented about 30 per cent of the total student population at all of the accredited American colleges of pharmacy. The number of women pharmacists and their percentage in this profession is rising rapidly.

Pharmacists are vital members of the health team. They carefully and meticulously dispense drugs and medicines as prescribed by physicians. There are many medicines that can be purchased from a drugstore without prescriptions; pharmacists are knowledgeable about these medicines and supply them and advise their customers on their use.

A great many drugs in their usable form now come to the drugstores directly from the drug manufacturers. Some medicines, however, are compounded by the pharmacists themselves; this means the pharmacists mix the ingredients to make the solutions, powders, capsules or other forms in which the medicines will ultimately be used by the patient.

There is a good deal of variation in the entrance requirements and curricula of the accredited colleges of pharmacy. A minimum of five years of post–high school education is needed in order to become a pharmacist. After the successful completion of a five-year program of studies, the graduate of an accredited college of pharmacy is awarded a bachelor of science (B.S.) in pharmacy or a bachelor of pharmacy (B. Pharm.) degree. Some colleges of pharmacy require the completion of six-year programs and award their graduates the doctor of pharmacy (Pharm. D.) degree. Those who aspire to careers in pharmacy should determine, while they are still in high school, the specific requirements of the college of pharmacy they would like to attend; some colleges of pharmacy accept students directly from high school and offer them a combined program of prepharmacy courses plus the professional training, whereas others permit the students to complete their prepharmacy courses elsewhere at an approved junior college, college or university.

Graduates of accredited colleges of pharmacy must pass a state board examination and, in almost all states, must complete a prescribed internship in order to obtain a license to practice.

In 1972, approximately 90 per cent of the licensed pharmacists worked in retail pharmacies; about half of this number were self-employed as *retail druggists,* as either partners or sole owners of their pharmacies, and the others were salaried employees in drugstores and community pharmacies. Most of the remainder were employed in hospitals as *hospital pharmacists* or by drug manufacturers as *medical sales representatives* (often known as *detail men*). The latter sell medicines to retail pharmacists and inform medical practitioners about the new drugs produced by the drug manufacturers for whom they work.

A much greater percentage of women than men work as hospital pharmacists than as retail pharmacists. A very small number of women work as "detail men."

Pharmacists must have interest and ability in science and health studies. They especially need to have a sense of integrity and responsibility and be accurate and dependable in dispensing medicines and filling prescriptions.

Women who are interested in the healing arts and in helping the ailing and who are able to instill confidence in others, so that customers and all with whom they have professional contact will trust them with their prescriptions, should seriously consider a career in this profession. This is a profession which has shown little discrimination against women and, today, certainly has a welcome mat out for them.

The demand for pharmacists exceeds the supply, and with increasing numbers of health insurance programs covering the payment of prescription drugs, the need for pharmacists will intensify. Women should find a bright employment future ahead of them in the field of pharmacy; additionally, to facilitate combining career and family responsibilities, there are excellent opportunities for part-time employment.

Further information about careers in pharmacy and a list of

71

the colleges of pharmacy may be obtained from the American Pharmaceutical Association, 2215 Constitution Ave. N.W., Washington, D.C. 20037.

Kappa Epsilon Fraternity, the national professional fraternity for women in pharmacy, has published two booklets about the opportunities for women in pharmacy. For copies and further information, write to Judith Ozbun, Secretary, Kappa Epsilon Fraternity, Inc., Executive Office, College of Pharmacy, North Dakota State University, Fargo, N.D. 58102.

Lambda Kappa Sigma is the "International Professional Fraternity for Women in Pharmacy." Further information about this professional fraternity may be obtained from Frances Curran, Grand Secretary, Lambda Kappa Sigma, 4509 Regent St., Philadelphia, Pa. 19143.

Podiatrists (also known as *chiropodists*) provide complete foot care to their patients. They numbered about 7,000 in 1970. About 5 per cent (approximately 350) were women.

Podiatrists diagnose and treat deformities and diseases of the feet. They may prescribe and use drugs, fit corrective devices and, when necessary, perform foot surgery. They refer their patients to physicians when they detect conditions requiring medical attention.

Colleges of podiatric medicine require two years of undergraduate college, including prescribed prepodiatric courses for admission. Graduates of a four-year podiatry program in an accredited college of podiatric medicine receive the doctor of podiatric medicine (D.P.M.) degree. After passing the required state board examination and receiving a license to practice podiatry, almost all of the graduates open their own offices and go into private practice.

People are living longer, and our population includes a rising number of older people, who more often need foot care and qualify for certain podiatric services under Medicare. This, added to the foot care problems of young people, will result in a growing demand for the services of podiatrists. The employment outlook is, therefore, favorable.

Women who have manual dexterity, scientific aptitude and an interest in foot care should give consideration to a career in podiatry. Women podiatrists are needed, and those who can empathize, communicate and relate well with elderly patients should find an especially great demand for their services.

For the names and addresses of the colleges of podiatric medicine and further career information, write to the American Podiatry Association, 20 Chevy Chase Circle N.W., Washington, D.C. 20015.

Hospital administrators are important members of the health service team, for they administer and coordinate the activities of hospital personnel to provide the best possible care for the patients. In 1970, there were approximately 17,000 hospital administrators; it was estimated that about 15 per cent of these administrators and their assistants were women.

All of the administrative activities of the hospital are managed by the hospital administrator, who generally works in close cooperation with the governing board of the hospital. In a limited number of hospitals, the administrators are physicians or nurses or, when the hospital is church-affiliated, they may be members of religious orders.

Those who hope to become hospital administrators should complete a four-year undergraduate college program, preferably with a major in business administration, and receive the bachelor's degree. They should then proceed to graduate school and enter an accredited master's degree program in hospital administration. These programs vary with the college or university offering them. Generally, they take two years to complete and consist of one year of classroom studies and one year of residency training in a hospital or health agency.

Hospital administrators should be able to get along well with people of all sorts and be tactful, good organizers and interested in helping those who are sick or injured. As time goes on, more women will be entering this occupation. Those who have the master's degree in hospital administration should find very good opportunities to start as *assistant hospital administrators* and then advance to full-fledged administrators.

For additional information about this profession and a list of the colleges and universities offering accredited master's degree programs in hospital administration, write to the American College of Hospital Administrators, 840 N. Lake Shore Drive, Chicago, Ill. 60611.

Sanitarians, as members of the health team, are specialists in environmental health. They are also known as *environmentalists.* The number of women in this field is tiny; of the approximately 15,000 sanitarians, women are estimated to be less than 1 per cent.

Sanitarians plan, manage and execute all aspects of environmental health programs. They are concerned about the cleanliness of the air we breathe, the water, milk and other liquids we drink, the food we eat and all other facets of the broad range of our environmental problems. They inspect dairies, restaurants, sewage disposal plants, swimming pools, water supplies and other places for possible health hazards. The majority of sanitarians work for government health agencies; others are employed by hospitals and food manufacturers and processors.

Four years of college leading to a bachelor's degree in public health, environmental health or a basic science are needed to obtain a beginner's position in this field. Graduate study leading to a master's degree in environmental health is recommended to advance as a sanitarian.

Mechanical aptitude to operate the testing devices used by sanitarians, ability and interest in health and science, tact and the ability to communicate effectively with those involved in the correction of unsanitary conditions are desirable characteristics for those who would like to become sanitarians. Many women possess these qualifications, and they are urgently needed in this field. The need for sanitarians is great, and it is anticipated that employment opportunities for those trained in this field will continue to be very favorable.

For further information about careers in environmental health, write to the American Public Health Association, 1740 Broadway, New York, N.Y. 10019, and the International Association of Milk, Food and Environmental Sanitarians, P.O. Box 437, Shelbyville, Ind. 46176.

Fairly new additions to the health team are the *inhalation therapists,* also known as *oxygen-therapy technicians.* They treat patients with respiratory (breathing) problems. In 1970, there were approximately 10,000 inhalation therapists, most of whom were at work in anesthesiology and pulmonary medicine departments of hospitals. The vast majority of them were men who had received on-the-job training.

As we entered into the 1970s, formalized academic programs began to replace on-the-job training in the field of inhalation therapy. Additionally, piped-in oxygen began to replace the heavy cylinders of gas in hospitals. The fact that it is no longer necessary to handle these heavy cylinders has contributed, at least in part, to the entry of women into this field.

In 1972, there were 313 actively employed registered female inhalation therapists. To administer oxygen and other gases to patients, as directed by the physicians, these therapists set up and operate such varied types of oxygen equipment as iron lungs, oxygen tents, incubators and resuscitators. They play vital roles in bringing relief to patients with illnesses such as chronic asthma, emphysema and other lung disorders, many of which are caused or aggravated by air pollution, and in the emergency treatment of acute breathing disturbances.

The American Registry of Inhalation Therapists is sponsored by the American Association for Inhalation Therapy, the American College of Chest Physicians and the American Society of Anesthesiologists. To become a registered inhalation therapist, the candidate must complete formal training plus one year of supervised experience and pass oral and written examinations. The formal training varies in length and may range from a two-year inhalation therapy program leading to an associate degree to a four-year bachelor's degree program including the required inhalation therapy courses. In 1972, there were 1,541 *registered* inhalation therapists.

Inhalation therapists should always be aware of the responsibility which rests upon them and must work with care and pay keen attention to detail. They must understand the needs of their patients, follow instructions meticulously and have mechanical aptitude. The need and demand for inhalation therapists are great and the employment outlook is excellent. Women therapists are urgently needed to perform these essential functions.

Details about training programs and registration requirements may be obtained from the American Registry of Inhalation Therapists, Office of the Executive Director, University of Rochester, Medical Center, Rochester, N.Y. 14642.

There are many health service occupations which have long been predominantly female and which will continue to provide women with excellent employment opportunities for many years to come. Nursing, as mentioned at the start of this chapter, is the largest of these occupations. Inasmuch as some of you may be interested in one or more of these traditional careers, we will mention them here briefly and tell you where you can get additional information about them.

Unlike the inhalation therapists, the vast majority of whom are male, females predominate among many of the other kinds of therapists and technicians in the health field.

The *electroencephalographic technicians,* popularly known as *EEG technicians,* attach electrodes to the patient's head to connect him to the electroencephalography machine; this produces an electroencephalogram, a "picture" of the electrical currents of

76

the patient's brain, which helps the physician to determine the presence of any brain disorders. Almost all of the EEG technicians are women; in 1970, there were about 3,000 EEG technicians.

Electrocardiograph technicians, usually called *EKG technicians,* take and process electrocardiograms as directed by a physician. The electrocardiograms, tracings produced by an electrocardiograph, are "pictures" of the patient's heartbeat and aid the physician in diagnosing the condition of the patient's heart. Most EKG technicians are women; there were approximately 9,500 EKG technicians in 1970. For further information about the careers of the EEG and EKG technicians, write to the American Hospital Association, 840 N. Lake Shore Drive, Chicago, Ill. 60611.

Occupational therapists plan, organize and participate in hospital occupational programs designed to rehabilitate mentally and physically ill patients. In consultation with physicians and other health specialists in the hospital, they plan educational, vocational and recreational activities for these patients. In 1970, there were approximately 7,500 occupational therapists in the United States, and more than 90 per cent of them were women. Write to the American Occupational Therapy Association, 251 Park Ave. South, New York, N.Y. 10010, for further information.

Physical therapists use such physical means as exercise, electricity, heat, light, massage and water to treat patients with bone, joint, muscle and nerve injuries or diseases. As members of a hospital health team, under the direction of a physician, they develop programs for treatment to help the patients overcome their disabilities. There were about 15,000 physical therapists throughout the country in 1970, of whom about 11,000 were women. For details about this profession, write to the American Physical Therapy Association, 1740 Broadway, New York, N.Y 10019.

Radiological technologists (popularly known until quite recently, and often still called, *medical x-ray technicians*) operate x-ray equipment. Under the direction of physicians, they apply radioactive substances and roentgen rays to patients for diagnostic and therapeutic purposes. There were about 55,000 female radiological technologists at work in 1970 out of a total number of about 80,000 radiological technologists. Details about this occupation may be obtained from the American Society of Radiological Technologists, 645 N. Michigan Ave., Chicago, Ill. 60611.

Almost all of the *medical assistants* (about 175,000) in 1970 were women. Medical assistants perform routine tasks to help physicians examine and treat patients. They keep the examination, consulting and waiting rooms in orderly, clean condition. Write to the American Association of Medical Assistants, 200 E. Ohio St., Chicago, Ill. 60611, for further information.

There are a variety of *medical laboratory workers,* and they perform miscellaneous tests under the supervision of physicians. *Medical technologists,* who have completed four years of college with appropriate medical technology courses and earned the bachelor's degree, perform numerous bacteriological, chemical, microscopic and other medical examinations to assist physicians in the diagnosis and treatment of disease. In 1970, it was estimated that about 80 to 90 per cent of the 110,000 medical laboratory workers were women. If you would like further information, write to the American Society of Medical Technologists, Suite 1600, Hermann Professional Bldg., Houston, Tex. 77025.

Medical record librarians compile and maintain records and reports on the illnesses and treatments of patients in clinics, hospitals and other institutions; they should not be confused with the *medical librarians,* who work with books, medical journals and other publications in the hospital libraries. Most of the medical record librarians (and medical librarians too) are women. Further information may be obtained from the American Medical Record Association, 875 N. Michigan Ave., Chicago, Ill. 60611.

rgest field of professional employment for women is
y teaching (including kindergarten teaching). There
e than 1,200,000 elementary school teachers at work
he 1970–71 school year and women far outnumbered

be stated here, however, that those who are preparing
ntary school teaching positions in the 1970s will find
petition for job openings. Employment opportunities in
itional field for women are diminishing, and it is an-
that in 1980 the enrollments in kindergartens and ele-
schools will be even lower than the 1970 levels.

who are trained to become *teachers of handicapped*
teachers of mentally retarded children and *teachers of*
taged children in the urban ghettos should not find it
to obtain employment throughout the 1970s. However,
ho had hoped to become elementary school teachers
without further specialty, will find it necessary to re-
eir thinking toward other career fields. If you are among
u should consider the many nontraditional opportunities
d to you in this book.

number of *secondary school teachers* employed in the
States during the 1970–71 school year exceeded 1,000,000;
1970–71, women held over half of the positions as *junior*
hool teachers and *senior high school teachers* throughout
ion.

e secondary schools too, it is anticipated that the supply
hers will exceed the demand with the exception of those
e trained to be *physical science teachers*. The demand
se should be favorable; additionally, there will be some
phic areas where the employment outlook for secondary
teachers will be favorable in the years ahead. In the main,
er, many young women who aspire to secondary school
g careers may find it necessary to enter other fields in-

Dietitians plan and direct the food service programs in hospitals and other institutions. They plan nutritious meals to help the patients recover and maintain good health. Women constituted more than 90 per cent of the 30,000 dietitians in the United States in 1970. For further information about careers in dietetics, write to the American Dietetics Association, 620 N. Michigan Ave., Chicago, Ill. 60611.

Speech and hearing are interrelated and *speech pathologists* and *audiologists* are generally classed together, for they must be knowledgeable in both occupations. The speech pathologist diagnoses, treats and performs research related to speech, language and voice problems of children and adults. The audiologist evaluates and treats hearing problems of children and adults. In 1970, it was estimated that there were about 22,000 speech pathologists and audiologists, of whom about 75 per cent were women. Details about careers in these two professions may be obtained from the American Speech and Hearing Association, 9030 Old Georgetown Road, Washington, D.C. 20014.

Many of the occupations discussed in this chapter, as you probably have already noted, offer the practitioners the opportunity to become self-employed. Those who decide upon self-employment should learn about business procedures and management, for although they are members of a specific profession, if they work for themselves, they are also in business and, no matter how knowledgeable they may be about their profession, if they do not know how to operate a business, they reduce their chances for success. See Chapter 9 for information about self-employment.

The demand for health personnel is so great that those who have need for financial aid in order to pay for the specialized training should have no difficulty obtaining this aid if they have the necessary preparation and qualifications to enter upon this training. The federal government has many grants available to help defray the expenses of those who wish to enter these "demand occupations"; many colleges and universities too offer scholarships and other tuition-free arrangements to members of minority groups, applicants who are financially disadvantaged and others whom these schools consider worthy of this help. Write to the professional association of your choice for information about financial aid opportunities in the specific occupation you would like to enter.

Occupations in the health fields will in all probability show continued rapid growth throughout the years ahead. Our nation's expanding population, increasing amounts of government expenditures for health care and services, growing coverage under prepayment programs for hospitalization and medical care, improved standards of living and greater awareness of the importance of good health care are among the many factors that will contribute to an increase in the demand for health services and consequent increase in the need for health personnel.

The future outlook for women in these healing arts fields is indeed bright.

Chapter 5

THE HELPING PROFESSIONS

EVE may have come from Adam and troubled, he probably wept that time, the shoulders of wom strength to strangers and friends

Today's woman can do more troubled people. She can be train fessions and become qualified to competent counseling. As we proc of the helping professions are inter

Teachers are the first professiona into contact upon their entry into *elementary school teachers,* althou pleted courses in child developmen educators and not counselors. Howe lieve that these professionals should as teachers, and surely they do offer and primary graders as they start way along their paths to the upper

Of all the professions, teaching is mately 2,600,000 members in the schools and colleges and universities th during the 1970–71 school year.

Since elementary school and secondary school teaching are traditional fields for women, we will not go into detail about them here. Those who would like further information about these careers should write to the American Federation of Teachers, 1012 14th St. N.W., Washington, D.C. 20005, and/or the National Education Association, 1201 16th St. N.W., Washington, D.C. 20036.

Although women outnumber men as elementary and secondary school teachers, it is noteworthy that men predominate as *district superintendents, school administrators* and *principals,* and in other administrative posts in public and private and parochial schools throughout the United States. This is the result of discriminatory practices in promotional procedures and not at all due to lack of qualifications on the part of the many experienced, competent women teachers.

The licensed *school counselors* (known too as *guidance counselors*) in the elementary and secondary schools are the professionals who have been trained to help young people to cope with their problems. On the elementary school level, these counselors are often called *adjustment counselors.* The pupils who come to the adjustment counselors and the students who come to the secondary school counselors are called counselees.

Counselors aim to help pupils cope with their problems in positive, productive fashion, and increase their understanding of themselves and the world around them. Pupils visit their counselor's office of their own volition with all types of problems, or are sent there by their teachers or school principal.

Guidance is a comparatively young profession and, therefore, the nature of the work of school counselors is still quite flexible. The counselor's activities may vary according to geographic area, nature of the student body, grade levels and type of school programs. School counselors are concerned with the educational, vocational, emotional and social development of their students. They assist the students in coping with their school problems

83

and with personal, social, family and home situations which may affect their school work and educational progress. Counselors strive to help students make the best possible use of their potential.

Students sometimes confuse counselors with *advisers*. Advisers give advice to the students, such as telling a student it would be better for him to take business arithmetic than algebra. School counselors help the students to help themselves. Counselors may also give advice, but essentially they offer guidance to enable the students themselves to make their own ultimate decisions.

Counselors offer individual and group educational and vocational guidance services. They may also administer psychological tests to determine the aptitudes, intelligence, interests and personality characteristics of their counselees for educational and vocational planning purposes.

In large school systems and large schools, counselors may advance to the position of *director of guidance* and have other school counselors, *grade advisers, college advisers* and *placement counselors* as assistants. *Grade advisers* generally assist students with their programs. *College advisers* aid juniors and seniors in high school in selecting the colleges they would like to attend and in gaining admission into them. *Placement counselors* help the students to obtain part-time, afterschool and full-time summer jobs. In smaller schools, one counselor may perform all of these functions.

The exact number of school counselors is not known because there are many teachers working part-time as counselors; some of these teachers are licensed to serve as counselors and some have only their teaching licenses. It is estimated, however, that in 1971, there were about 54,000 licensed school counselors. More than 80 per cent of them were employed in public secondary schools; about 10 per cent worked in public elementary schools and the remainder in private schools, parochial schools and other educational institutions.

84

It is not known exactly how many women there are among the school counselors in the schools throughout the nation. However, men definitely are in the majority, and men also far outnumber women as directors of guidance and *supervisors of guidance* in the school systems of the large cities.

You have probably consulted your school counselor at least once during your high school years. Perhaps as a result, you have decided you would like to become a counselor. In most states, to become a counselor, one must first be a teacher. Thus, if you aspire to a career as a school counselor in a state which requires teaching experience, you need to take the regular teacher education program in college, acquire the prescribed teaching experience and complete the required counselor education graduate program toward the master's degree before or while teaching. In an increasing number of states, a counseling internship as part of the master's degree counselor education program is replacing the need for teaching experience.

The requirements for certification as a school counselor vary from state to state, and many recent changes have occurred and continue to take place. It is advisable that you write to the Department of Education in the state capital of the state in which you would like to work to determine its specific requirements. Counselors who would like to advance to positions as directors or supervisors of guidance are advised to obtain the Ph.D. degree in guidance or psychology.

If you like to work with young people in a school setting and would like to help them achieve their greatest possible potential educationally and vocationally, then guidance may be the field for you.

The present ratio of counselors to students in most schools throughout the country is far below the generally accepted standards. The need for counselors is great, and employment opportunities are expected to be favorable throughout the remainder of the 1970s and into the 1980s. The warmth and wisdom of women are needed in the guidance field, and a wholehearted welcome awaits you if you have the preparation and qualifications needed to become a member of this field.

For further details about careers in guidance and a list of colleges and universities offering counselor education programs, write to the American Personnel and Guidance Association, 1607 New Hampshire Ave. N.W., Washington, D.C. 20009, and to the American School Counselor Association, a division of the American Personnel and Guidance Association, at the same address.

As this writer stated at the start of this chapter, many of the helping professions and the healing arts professions are closely related. There are some unusual women who have achieved success in two or more of these related professions. Dr. Essie E. Lee, Director of Student Affairs, Division of Student Services, Institute of Health Sciences of Hunter College of the City University of New York, in New York City, and author of *Careers in the Health Field* (Messner, 1972), is an excellent example of such a woman.

Dr. Lee says: "From as far back as I care to remember, I have always had an interest in people, all kinds of people—children, adults, the elderly. I suppose it was my mother's influence. She was a great humanitarian and affiliated with every local cause devoted to the relief of sickness and suffering. After high school, I selected the field of teaching and entered Smith College to major in biology. But success in liberal arts did not bring any great sense of satisfaction, so I embarked upon a nursing career. After several years of bedside nursing, I enrolled at New York University to study another kind of nursing, public health nursing."

"Public health nursing," continues Dr. Lee, "affords greater opportunity for working independently and with little direct supervision. As part of my assignment, I served as the school nurse in a junior high school that had classes for orthopedically handicapped children. The more I observed these fantastically independent youngsters, the more I admired their courage and tenacity. Later, I returned to New York University to earn a certificate in physical therapy. Working with the handicapped is truly challenging. But after five years, the old restlessness returned, and I found myself thinking about teaching."

Dr. Lee continues on to explain her entry into the field of guidance and student personnel administration. "For the next three years," she says, "I taught general science, hygiene and biology to vocational high school girls. But, somehow, I was not fulfilled and decided to earn a professional diploma or certificate in Guidance at City College. Since I spent so much time helping people, I decided to earn the credentials. As everyone knows, nothing succeeds like success, and so, having completed requirements for the advanced certificate (the first ever granted at City College), I felt compelled to continue toward my doctorate. I registered for courses toward this degree at Teachers College, Columbia University, from which I had earned my M.A. degree in health education."

"Meanwhile," explains Dr. Lee, "I served as guidance counselor in vocational and academic high schools, as consultant to the Bureau of Guidance of the New York City Board of Education and as Coordinator of the College Discovery Program at Kingsborough Community College in Brooklyn. This program provided supportive services to academically and economically less privileged students. I worked hard, but the rewards were equally satisfying, and I remained long enough to see two classes graduate."

"The Institute of Health Sciences came into being in 1968," says Dr. Lee in regard to her present position. "It was the first unit of the City University of New York to offer the unique opportunity of earning undergraduate and graduate degrees in health areas. My appointment as Coordinator and later as Director of Student Affairs was the culmination of many years of education and experience, and my duties permitted me to use all facets of my previous training. I am responsible for personal, academic and career counseling, recruitment, admissions and referrals. My dual preparation, in the health sciences and in guidance, allows me to assume diverse duties and responsibilities, such as the evaluation of records and students' past educational experiences."

"It may seem to many that my career plans were unstable and constantly in a state of flux," Dr. Lee adds. "However, today most young people will find that basic skills need updating and revising each year. All of my education involved the 'helping' and health professions, so I found it easier to move from one to another. The basic interests in working with and helping people and the interest in scientific areas remained stable. I see it as building vertically and horizontally at the same time. If one wants to counsel and guide students in a health-oriented setting, some health background is necessary to understand the problems, difficulties and joys that one encounters."

On the college and university level, there are various *student personnel specialists* who help the students to resolve their problems satisfactorily. In addition to the *director of student affairs*, discussed in the preceding paragraphs by Dr. Essie Lee, there are the *admissions officers* and *directors of admissions*, who are involved with the recruitment, selection and admission of students who appear to be qualified for admission to their institution; the *college advisers*, who assist the students with the selection of their courses, programming of classes and similar matters; and the *financial aid officers* and the *directors of financial aid*, who help those who have problems meeting their tuition and other expenses by advising them of the available scholarships, grants, loans, employment opportunities on and off campus and all other types of financial aids.

College placement officers are also classified under the heading of student personnel administration. They are known too as *college career planning and placement counselors*. They maintain job placement services for students and graduates of their college or university. These placement officers assist the students in obtaining part-time positions during the academic year and full-time positions for their summer vacation periods. They also aid graduates in finding beginner's positions in their chosen fields.

In 1972, there were about 3,000 college placement officers working in colleges and universities in the United States; approximately 25 per cent of them were women. The number of placement officers employed by the junior and community colleges is not available, but with the proliferation of these colleges, that number is increasing annually.

To obtain employment as a college placement officer or other student personnel administrator, a master's degree in student personnel administration is desirable. It is anticipated that the number of opportunities in this field will rise throughout the remainder of the 1970s and into the 1980s.

Further information about careers in student personnel administration is available from the American Personnel and Guidance Association, 1607 New Hampshire Ave. N.W., Washington, D.C. 20009, and the American College Personnel Association, a division of the American Personnel and Guidance Association, at the same address.

College and university faculty members (teachers) range from the *lecturers,* the beginners in the field of college teaching, to the top-level *full professors.* In between, there are the *instructors, assistant professors* and *associate professors.* There were somewhat more than 330,000 full-time college teachers in American colleges and universities for the 1970–71 academic year; additionally, more than 150,000 taught on a part-time basis.

Men far outnumber women as college and university teachers. More than 90 per cent of the faculty members of the schools of law, engineering and agriculture and the physical sciences departments are men; women predominate as teachers of home economics, library science and nursing.

On an over-all basis, women represent about 20 per cent of the college and university teachers. However, these female faculty members are, in the main, clustered in the lower ranks as lecturers, instructors and assistant professors, and found principally in community colleges, small four-year colleges and the less prestigious universities. In the major universities, women represent only about 2 per cent of the full professors.

During 1972, women faculty members in many colleges and universities and in many of the individual departments grouped together to form task forces, women's caucuses, women's coalitions, committees on the status of women and the like to fight what they called "gross discrimination" against women in these institutions of higher education. The "weapon" they used in their fight is Executive Order 11246 as amended by Order 11375, forbidding discrimination on the basis of sex by institutions which have federal contracts; colleges and universities have in recent years become large scale federal contractors. This Executive Order states "the contractor shall not discriminate against any employee or applicant for employment because of race, color, religion, sex or national origin."

If you would like to teach someday in a college or university, your ability to obtain such a position and to advance to upper ranks of professorships will hopefully be easier because of the battles being waged today by women faculty members on campuses throughout the nation. College professorships on a part-time basis are particularly attractive positions for professional women who are married and have children.

To become a college teacher, you must be a specialist in a particular subject field. The master's degree in that subject field is required for a beginner's position and the doctor's degree is generally required for advancement into the professorship levels. Women who wish to become college professors will probably find competition for these positions rather keen in the years ahead. Competition, however, will vary with each subject field and in some fields employment prospects for those who have their Ph.D.s will be more favorable than in others.

For information on college teaching employment opportunities in a particular subject field, write to the professional association of that specific field. Additionally, further information on a career in college teaching may be obtained from the American Association of University Professors, 1 DuPont Circle, Suite 500, Washington, D.C. 20036, and the American Council on Education, 1 DuPont Circle, Washington, D.C. 20036.

Other members of the helping professions are the *employment counselors*. Employment counselors generally assist persons who are no longer attending school. They are known too as *vocational counselors*. Those who come to them for assistance are often called clients. These clients are offered help in planning their career goals on the basis of their background and potential. Employment counselors also assist their clients in finding and entering appropriate training programs, when training is necessary, and aid them in locating suitable employment when they are ready for employment.

The specific nature of the work of employment counselors depends upon the agency by whom they are employed. About 70 per cent of them work in state employment service offices; these employment service offices may be found in every large city and many smaller ones throughout the nation. The remainder are employed by community agencies, private agencies, training schools and other institutions, and the Veterans Administration and other federal agencies.

Men had been in the majority in the field of employment counseling until quite recently. However, there were approximately 9,000 such counselors at work in 1972, and about half of them were women, so a 50-50 ratio of male-to-female employment counselors appears to have been achieved.

The minimum educational requirement for entry into this field is the bachelor's degree with major study in one of the social sciences plus the completion of courses in counseling, vocational guidance and personnel administration on the undergraduate or graduate level. The master's degree in vocational counseling or a related field is generally required for advancement in this field.

The job future appears to be very bright for qualified employment counselors. It is expected that the number of these counselors in the state employment service offices will increase very rapidly throughout the remainder of the 1970s, especially as these counselors will not only aid unemployed clients to find employment, but also assist underemployed persons to obtain more appropriate positions.

Further details on careers in employment counseling or vocational counseling are available from the American Personnel and Guidance Association, 1607 New Hampshire Ave. N.W., Washington, D.C. 20009, and the National Employment Counselors Association and the National Vocational Guidance Association, both of which are divisions of the American Personnel and Guidance Association, at the same address.

Rehabilitation counselors work chiefly with the physically and mentally disabled. Since the mid-1960s, many rehabilitation counselors have also been working with the socially disadvantaged. The vocational and personal adjustment of these disabled persons is the concern of these counselors. Rehabilitation counselors stress that it is what the disabled person can do, and not what he can't do, that counts.

Many of these counselors specialize in an area of rehabilitation which holds a particular interest for them. Thus, there are those who work solely with the blind; others work exclusively with alcoholics, emotionally disturbed, orthopedically disabled or some other group of disabled children or adults. Generally, the rehabilitation counselor works as a member of a team with physicians, psychologists, social workers, physical therapists, occupational therapists and other specialists to develop a plan of rehabilitation for the best possible personal, educational and vocational progress of the disabled person.

Approximately one-third of all the rehabilitation counselors are women. In 1970, there were about 13,000 rehabilitation counselors at work in the United States. About 75 per cent of them worked in state and local rehabilitation agencies; hospitals, insurance companies, sheltered workshops, special schools and varied other private and public agencies that had rehabilitation programs employed the remainder.

The master's degree in rehabilitation counseling or in a related discipline, such as social work or psychology, is desirable for entrance into this field. The doctorate in rehabilitation counseling or counseling psychology is generally required for advancement to supervisory or higher administrative positions in rehabilitation agencies.

If you would like to help the disabled to cope with their problems and live productive lives, you can do so by becoming a member of this profession. You should receive much gratification from your work as a rehabilitation counselor. There is a shortage of qualified counselors. Women who are trained to enter this field will find a warm welcome and very good employment opportunities available to them throughout the 1970s.

For additional information on careers in rehabilitation counseling, write to the American Rehabilitation Counseling Association, 1607 New Hampshire Ave. N.W., Washington, D.C. 20009, and the National Rehabilitation Counseling Association, 1522 K St. N.W., Washington, D.C. 20005.

Social work and psychology, as stated three paragraphs earlier, are disciplines related to rehabilitation counseling.

Social worker is an umbrella title applied to a large group of professionals who perform a variety of social service functions in a public or voluntary social welfare agency, organization, hospital, institution or school. Most *social workers* provide a

NONTRADITIONAL CAREERS FOR WOMEN

miscellany of social services directly to individuals, families or groups.

Caseworkers assist and counsel individuals and families who need the help of the social service agency. *Group workers* use varied group techniques and activities to help people better understand themselves and their problems and thus improve their way of life. There are *medical social workers,* who aid patients and their families in hospitals and related health centers; *psychiatric social workers,* who help patients with mental and emotional disturbances; and *school social workers,* who work with schoolchildren, their parents and their teachers.

Although beginners' jobs in the field of social work may be obtained by those who have solely the bachelor's degree, to be considered a professional social worker, one must have the master's degree in social work.

The employment future for professional social workers appears to be very bright. The demand for social workers is expected to be great, owing in large part to the complexities of our urban societies, weakening of family ties and increasing population of the very young and the very old, the two age groups generally most in need of special social services. Qualified, experienced female social workers who would like to combine career and family should find many part-time positions available to them.

Social work has traditionally been a woman's field and women continue to predominate in this profession, although an increasing number of men have begun to enter it. The vast majority of the approximately 170,000 social workers who worked in government and other agencies throughout the nation in 1970 were women. Therefore, we will not go into any further detail about this profession here. Those who would like additional information should write to the National Association of Social Workers, 2 Park Avenue, New York, N.Y. 10016.

Psychologists are concerned about why people, individually and in groups, behave as they do. Their aim is to help people

94

cope with their problems. Women are more apt to go to psychologists with their problems than are men, and many women have expressed a preference for discussing their problems with a female psychologist rather than with a male psychologist. Yet only 25 per cent of the estimated 40,000 psychologists who were at work in the United States in 1970 were women.

The field of psychology has many interrelated branches, and most psychologists specialize in one of these branches. *Clinical psychologists* generally strive to ease the problems of emotionally and mentally disturbed patients in clinics, mental hospitals and other institutions; they administer diagnostic tests and provide individual and group programs of treatment as they may deem necessary.

Counseling psychologists, in the main, serve normal people and assist them in arriving at satisfactory adjustments to their personal, social, educational, occupational or other problems; they too administer and interpret psychological tests and employ individual and group counseling techniques as each situation may warrant.

Experimental psychologists work in laboratories, where they conduct experiments to study problems in human and animal behavior; they write reports describing these experiments and interpreting the results to help other psychologists in their work. *Industrial psychologists* develop and supply psychological techniques to the selection and training and the improvement of morale and motivation of employees in industry.

School psychologists work in cooperation with the school counselors. They administer psychological tests, diagnose the needs of individual children and plan corrective programs to enable these children to achieve better educational performance and more effective adjustment in school. *Social psychologists* study human relationships and analyze the social forces which affect the behavior of human beings.

The minimum educational requirement for some beginner's

positions in this field is the master's degree in psychology. The Ph.D. degree is becoming increasingly desirable and, in some cases, necessary, for many entrance positions and is definitely necessary for the more responsible clinical, counseling and research positions and for advancement into higher level positions.

The Ph.D. is also important for those who wish to become self-employed, independent practitioners. Most states require that those who conduct a private practice as a psychologist must be certified or licensed by the state in which they practice. Specific requirements for certification or licensing in a particular state may be obtained from the department of education located in the capital of that state.

Do you enjoy helping people? Are you interested in the well-being of people? Do you have patience toward people with problems? Are you known for your sensitivity, warmth, maturity, sense of responsibility and emotional stability? If so, a career in psychology may be compatible with your attributes. As a woman, if you acquire the necessary educational preparation, you should find a warm welcome in this field.

Most psychologists work in colleges and universities. Others work in government agencies, such as the Veterans Administration and the Public Health Service, and in public and private schools, industry, clinics, community health centers, hospitals and various other institutions. Some psychologists have their own independent practices.

The future looks bright indeed for competent, qualified psychologists. Excellent employment opportunities are anticipated through the 1970s for those who have the Ph.D. degree. Additional information about careers in psychology is available from the American Psychological Association, 1200 17th St. N.W., Washington, D.C. 20036.

The social sciences are related to psychology and social work and come under the broad umbrella of the fields of human relationships. They cover all aspects of human society. The *social scientists* include *anthropologists, economists, geographers, historians, political scientists* and *sociologists.*

Anthropologists concentrate on the study of primitive tribes, the origins of people and the civilizations and cultures of the past. They make comparative studies of the origins, evolution and races of human beings.

There were about 3,500 anthropologists in the United States in 1972, and about 25 per cent of them were women. Although the present number of female anthropologists is small, it is interesting to note that one of the foremost anthropologists of all time is a woman, Dr. Margaret Mead.

The master's degree in anthropology is required for most beginner's positions in this field; the Ph.D. is necessary for advancement to higher posts. Anthropologists are employed in colleges and universities, museums, archeological research programs, health research projects and federal agencies.

Increasing opportunities are opening up for women in anthropology, and the employment outlook appears to be favorable for the remainder of the 1970s. If you are fascinated by diggings and expeditions, have an above-average interest in natural history, like to travel and believe you could cope with the disadvantages of remote work areas, you might like to get further information about careers in anthropology. To do so, write to the American Anthropological Association, 1703 New Hampshire Ave. N.W., Washington, D.C. 20009.

Economists conduct research, prepare reports and formulate plans to help solve economic problems that arise from the production and distribution of goods and services. Economics, the largest of the social science fields, had about 33,000 members in 1972. They worked for business and industrial firms, colleges and universities, private research organizations and federal agencies. For beginner's positions, the bachelor's degree with a major in economics is sufficient. The master's degree is desirable for advancement.

NONTRADITIONAL CAREERS FOR WOMEN

The American Economic Association in 1972 established a Committee on the Status of Women in the Economics Profession. The primary goal of this committee is the elimination of discrimination in the economics field. Employment opportunities for women in this field are improving and the outlook is very favorable for those who have graduate degrees in economics. For further information, write to Helen B. Munzer, Executive Secretary, Committee on the Status of Women in the Economics Profession, 131 Kent St., Brookline, Mass. 02146, and/or the American Economic Association, Suite 812, Oxford House, 1313 21st Avenue South, Nashville, Tenn. 37212.

Geographers study the nature and use of areas of the earth's surface. They conduct research studies on the physical and climatic aspects of certain areas and regions and relate these to the changing patterns of where people live. Most of the estimated 7,100 geographers, of whom women represented about 12 per cent in 1972, were employed by colleges and universities and federal agencies.

The bachelor's degree is the minimum requirement for entrance into this field. There are good employment prospects for geographers, especially for those with graduate degrees. Further information about careers in this field may be obtained from the Society of Women Geographers, 1619 New Hampshire Ave. N.W., Washington, D.C. 20009, and/or the Association of American Geographers, 1710 16th St. N.W., Washington, D.C. 20009.

There are favorable employment prospects for *historians, political scientists* and *sociologists* who have Ph.D. degrees in their respective fields.

Historians are concerned with records of events, ideas, institutions and people of the past; they prepare chronological accounts of past or current events dealing with some aspects of human activity. *Political scientists* study government; they conduct research into the development and operation of political institutions, study political behavior and develop political theories (see also *politicians* in Chapter 11). *Sociologists* study the origin, behavior, development and interaction of the groups which people form in their association with each other; they analyze the patterns of culture and social organization which have developed as a result of group life in society.

There were approximately 15,500 historians, 11,000 political scientists and 12,000 sociologists at work in 1970, and the vast majority were employed by colleges and universities and government agencies. The exact number of women in each of these fields is not available, but it is rather small.

For further information about these occupations, write to one or more of the following according to your individual interests:

American Historical Association
400 A St. S.E.
Washington, D.C. 20003

American Political Science Association
1527 New Hampshire Ave. N.W.
Washington, D.C. 20036

American Sociological Association
1722 N St. N.W.
Washington, D.C. 20036

There are not enough trained people to aid all those who need help with their problems. As a result, new careers have developed for *mental health paraprofessionals* to assist the professionals and thus enable the latter to help a greater number of troubled people than they otherwise could.

Mental health technicians and *human services technicians* are members of new career fields. Excellent opportunities for employment will be available to women who obtain the necessary preparation for these paraprofessions in the coming years. If you are compassionate, warm and tender and would like to help the mentally disturbed, mentally ill and/or mentally retarded, you can qualify for these positions by completing a two-year college program in mental health technology or any of the human services technology programs. There is a critical shortage of mental health personnel, and understanding women are urgently needed.

If you would like more details about these careers, write to the National Association for Mental Health, 1800 K. St., Rosslyn, Va. 22209, and the National Clearinghouse for Mental Health Information, U.S. Public Health Service, Health Services and Mental Health Administration, National Institute of Mental Health, 5600 Fishers Lane, Rockville, Md. 20852. For further information, you can consult this writer's book on paraprofessional careers, mentioned earlier.

Two new and developing professions in the field of mental health are art therapy and music therapy. *Art therapists* use art as an aid in the care and treatment of the mentally disturbed and the retarded. They help patients to express themselves by means of paintings, drawings and/or clay sculpture. *Music therapists* plan, direct and organize prescribed musical activities as part of the programs involving care and treatment of patients.

The *art therapists* and *music therapists* work in cooperation with the physicians and other members of the rehabilitation team. Since these professions are so young, the educational preparation required in each is not as yet uniform. These therapists should have art and music aptitude and training, respectively, and the bachelor's degree, including the successful completion of courses in art, music, psychology, mental health, rehabilitation and special education.

The future for women in these therapies appears to be very bright. If you would like further information about these careers and the names and addresses of the colleges and universities offering training in these fields, write to the American Art Therapy Association c/o Myra Levick, Hahnemann Medical College, Pittsburgh, Pa. 19102, and/or the National Association for Music Therapy, P.O. Box 610, Lawrence, Kans. 66044.

Members of the clergy are another large category of professionals who are concerned with the well-being of their fellow human beings. Certainly, the ministry is one of the helping professions, yet here is a field so predominantly male that a woman is indeed a rarity. "Clergywoman" is such a strange-sounding title because there are so few *clergywomen*.

There is no reason why women cannot do as competent a job in spiritually and otherwise helping members of their religious faith as men can do. Yet the doors of the ministry, priesthood and rabbinate have long had "men only" signs on them. Now women in Judeo-Christian sects are demanding that both sexes be permitted to participate equally in religious practices. They have become dissatisfied with being allowed only to serve tea at religious luncheons and are demanding the right to do more. In churches, temples and synagogues throughout the nation, women have begun to fight for equal opportunities and equal participation before God.

Women have succeeded in recent years in making a breakthrough in the Protestant ministry. Most of the major Protestant denominations now ordain women. Yet the number of these ordained women is still small; they also tend to receive the poorest job offerings and many have been unable to get church positions.

In 1972, there were about 300,000 Protestant ministers; of the 40,000 ministers in the United Methodist Church, approximately 300 were women; of the 13,000 ministers in the United Presbyterian Church, about ninety were women; and of the 9,000 ministers in the United Church of Christ, about forty were women. It was estimated that less than 3 per cent in the entire Protestant ministry were women. Increasing numbers of women are attending seminaries, and the number of women who are serving as *pastor's assistants* is also increasing in some Protestant denominations.

There were in 1972 approximately 60,000 *Roman Catholic priests* in the United States; there were no women priests. A decree by Pope Paul in September, 1972, continued to bar

101

Catholic women from even the smallest formal role in the ministry of the Roman Catholic church.

Judaism has three branches—Orthodox, Conservative and Reform. In 1972, there were about 6,500 *rabbis* in the United States. Most of these rabbis were members of the Orthodox branch of Judaism, the most traditional of the three branches. There were no women Orthodox or Conservative rabbis, for these two branches of Judaism do not permit women to become rabbis. In June, 1972, Sally Priesand became the first woman to be ordained as a rabbi in the United States; she is a member of the Reform branch of Judaism.

As time goes on, more and more women will be ordained, but in the more conservative, traditional religions, such as Roman Catholicism and Orthodox Judaism, it will probably be a long, long time before this takes place. Age-old traditions tend to give way much more slowly within the confines of religious institutions than in secular society. Religious traditions are older and firmer than other traditions, and one of these olden traditions is the Judeo-Christian concept of God as a patriarch and woman as lesser than man.

Actually, there is no Judeo-Christian theological basis for refusing to permit women to serve God and humanity as full-fledged members of the clergy. The practice of barring women from the ministry, priesthood and rabbinate reflects ancient concepts of women's place in society. These concepts have undergone tremendous changes in recent times.

So, if you would like to be ordained in the religion of your faith, whether you are Protestant, Catholic or Jewish, get all the theological training necessary—and, better yet, even more than necessary—and then be prepared to fight for your rights in your respective religious faiths.

As one woman recently said to me, "I prayed to God and *She* answered my prayers."

102

Chapter 6

WOMEN IN MATH AND SCIENCE

HAVE you had a teacher (or anyone else) tell you that math and science are not for girls? If so, you are not alone. You are a member of a very large "club."

For many years and up into the 1960s, there were high school teachers and college professors who warned their female students not to consider careers involving math and/or science. They insisted that these careers are for men only. This, of course, is utter nonsense.

Even at the start of the 1970s, there were those die-hard professors who continued to advise their female students to resist any thoughts they might have of careers in math or science. Fortunately, few professors with such antiquated ideas are any longer found in the colleges throughout the nation.

Of course, there are many women who do not have any mathematical or scientific aptitude or interest—and there are many men who do. But, conversely, there are many women who *do* have mathematical and scientific aptitude and interest and excel in these fields—and many, many men who do not!

Women are needed as mathematicians and scientists. At the start of the 1970s, there were conditions in the national labor market which caused many scientists and engineers to lose their jobs, and unemployment was a major concern in these fields.

However, in spite of such short-term employment fluctuations, projections indicate that the long-term outlook is very bright and that there will be rapid growth in these fields as we proceed toward 1980.

Let us look in on occupations in math and science that need women and will offer them many thousands of employment opportunities in the years ahead.

Many women find it challenging and exciting to work with numbers. Mathematics is an important tool in many fields, particularly in the scientific and engineering fields and also in the business world. Additionally, mathematics is a profession.

In the category of mathematics and related fields, the *mathematicians, actuaries* and *statisticians* are members of three occupations which need a far greater number of women than are now in them.

Mathematicians are involved with numbers in many ways, from the formulation of new theories to the translation of scientific and other problems into mathematical terms. In 1970, there were about 75,000 mathematicians at work in the United States (this included over 5,000 persons doing actuarial work, which will be discussed next). Women represented approximately 10 per cent of this number.

Mathematicians solve problems in various fields by using mathematical methods. They do all sorts of computations and do research in such branches of mathematics as algebra, geometry and calculus.

There are two broad divisions of mathematical activities. The *theoretical mathematicians* work in the area of pure or theoretical mathematics and aim to develop and discover new mathematical principles and relationships. The *applied mathematicians* employ math as a tool for solving practical problems, especially in the fields of science and engineering.

Mathematicians should have a logical mind, a sharp sense of curiosity, an ability and eagerness to solve problems and numerical aptitude. A bachelor's degree with a major in mathematics is the minimum requirement for starting positions in mathematics. Those who wish to advance to higher level positions should continue on to graduate school for their master's degree. The Ph.D. degree is desirable, and often necessary, to become a senior mathematician doing advanced research.

Most mathematicians work in private industry, primarily in aircraft and electrical equipment industries and in research and development firms; others are employed by colleges and universities and by government agencies.

There is a professional association for women that aims to improve the status of women in mathematics; most of its members are high school teachers and college professors of mathematics. If you would like further information, write to Prof. Mary Gray, Association for Women in Mathematics, American University, College of Arts and Sciences, Department of Mathematics and Statistics, Washington, D.C. 20016.

Women are needed in the field of mathematics. Employment opportunities, on a long-range basis, should be favorable for those who have graduate degrees. Additional information about careers in mathematics may be obtained from the Mathematical Association of America, 1225 Connecticut Ave. N.W., Washington, D.C. 20036.

Actuaries are classed with mathematicians, since their work is essentially mathematical in nature. In addition to their knowledge of math and statistics, they have studied the principles of finance and business. They use this knowledge to design insurance and pension programs and to maintain these programs on a sound financial basis. They decide on the contract provisions in many different types of insurance policies and determine what the premium rates should be.

In 1972, the Society of Actuaries had a membership of approximately 4,000 professional actuaries residing in the United States and Canada. These members are called "professional actuaries" because they successfully completed the entire series of examinations required for full professional status in this field. Additionally, there were a few thousand other persons with mathematical skills doing actuarial work in the United States.

It was estimated that women represented less than 3 per cent of the total number of actuaries. The number of female actuaries has been increasing in recent years. Among those who took the first examinations in the series administered by the Society of Actuaries in the early 1970s, it was found that about 20 to 25 per cent were females, indicating that the number of females in this field is continuing upward.

Entry into the field of actuarial work calls for a bachelor's degree with a good foundation in mathematics, statistics and business administration. Those who hope to become actuaries should take the beginning examinations of the series of tests required for full professional status while they are still at college; this will give them a headstart toward professional standing as an actuary.

Approximately 80 per cent of all actuaries are employed by private insurance companies; most of the rest work for consulting firms and rating bureaus. There is a shortage of actuaries, and the need for them is growing. It is anticipated that employment opportunities for qualified actuaries will be excellent throughout the 1970s. Women are welcome and wanted, and those with ability and interest in math and statistics should give consideration to this field of work.

For further information about careers in actuarial work, write to the Society of Actuaries, 209 S. LaSalle St., Chicago, Ill. 60604.

Statisticians work with numbers to describe a wide variety of situations. They plan and conduct surveys and collect, organize, interpret, summarize and analyze the numerical data they have obtained. They may present these data in tables and graphs and/or write reports describing this information. They may conduct surveys and analyze the data on varied aspects of population studies, business and economic conditions, physical science and engineering problems, public opinion, vital statistics and many other matters about which statistical information is desired.

There were approximately 24,000 statisticians in the United States in 1970, of whom approximately one-third were women. The major employer of statisticians is the federal government, followed by colleges and universities, research institutes and private industry.

A bachelor's degree with major study in statistics or mathematics is the minimum requirement for beginning positions in statistics. To advance as a statistician, a master's degree in statistics is desirable. The ability to translate problems and situations into statistical terms, training in logical thinking, mathematical aptitude and an interest in work with numbers are necessary for success as a statistician.

It is anticipated that there will be very good opportunities for employment in this field throughout the 1970s. We are a society that collects data. More and more data are being collected and interpreted, and more statisticians will be needed to do this work.

In 1972, the American Statistical Association established a Committee on Women in Statistics to improve the opportunities for women in this profession. There is also a Caucus for Women in Statistics, which is attempting to recruit more women into the field of statistics.

Dr. Jean D. Gibbons, Chairperson of the Committee on Women in Statistics, received her master's degree with major study in mathematics from Duke University and her Ph.D. in statistics from Virginia Polytechnic Institute. Although she is only in her thirties, she has already achieved considerable professional success and is the Chairman of the Department of Statistics and Quantitative Methods at the University of Alabama, College of Commerce and Business Administration.

Dr. Gibbons says: "I would highly recommend statistics as an exceptionally good field for girls to enter. Judging from my own experiences and from the number of women who have become well-known statisticians within the last twenty years, the barriers to women in our profession appear to be relatively few. On the contrary, in fact, since women tend to be good at organization and attention to detail, methodological and oriented toward logical thinking, they have a natural affinity for statistics."

"The most important aptitude and early training area is mathematics," stresses Dr. Gibbons, "since this is the foundation of all statistical procedures. My advice to prospective statisticians is to have a strong background and interest in mathematics, followed by specialized training in statistics. The present demand seems to imply a course of study which couples statistics training with some specified field of application, like biology, business, psychology, sociology, computer science, etc.

"My own background is as above except that I do not have any particular area of application. My employment experience has been limited to a university faculty, as this provides me with ample opportunity for independent research and writing, besides always gratifying classroom experiences and contact with students."

"Teaching," continues Dr. Gibbons, "has always been considered a good career for a female, but it is especially so at the college level if the career is combined with marriage and a family. A college teacher's schedule is very flexible, and a large portion of the work can be done at home. A Ph.D. is almost essential for a college teaching career, but it is well worth the time invested."

For additional information about careers in statistics, write to the American Statistical Association, 806 15th St. N.W., Washington, D.C. 20005.

The natural sciences encompass the environmental, life and physical sciences; they are concerned with the physical world and all the living beings and things in, on, over and surrounding it. There is a good deal of overlap in these branches of the field of natural science, and often scientists from one branch have a basic knowledge of the subject matter of the other branches.

Environmental science is the smallest branch of the natural sciences. Life science is next in size, and physical science is the largest of the three branches.

The *environmental scientists* include the *geologists, geophysicists, meteorologists* and *oceanographers.* Collectively, these scientists are involved with the earth and the characteristics and composition of its water, land, interior, atmosphere and space environment.

Geologists are concerned with the history, composition and structure of the crust of the earth. To identify and determine the order of different processes that affected the development of the earth, geologists examine rocks, minerals and fossil remains.

In 1970, there were about 23,000 geologists at work in this country; approximately 4 per cent of them were females. The majority were employed by private industry, mainly by petroleum and natural gas producers; others worked in government agencies, colleges and universities.

Geophysicists study the physical characteristics of the earth, including its atmosphere and hydrosphere. They measure and investigate seismic, gravitational, electrical, thermal and magnetic forces affecting the earth; to do these things, they use the principles of physics, mathematics and chemistry, plus many highly complex instruments.

Among the specialists in the field of geophysics are the *geodesists* and *seismologists. Geodesists* study the weight, size, shape and gravitational field of the earth. The accurate mapping of the earth's surface is a primary function of theirs; as man goes out further into space, geodesists will similarly study other celestial bodies. *Seismologists* study earthquakes and man-made explosions using a delicate instrument known as the seismograph.

The American Geophysical Union had about 10,000 members

in 1972, and approximately 1 per cent of them were women. Among new members, however, the percentage has been rising to about 2 per cent of the incoming membership. In the specialties concerned with space science, the percentage of women geophysicists has already risen to 3. The trend is toward increasing numbers of women in this science as colleges and universities are making more training programs available to female students. Most geophysicists are employed by private industry.

Meteorologists study and interpret atmospheric conditions and allied information to forecast immediate and long-range changes in the weather. They are concerned with all atmospheric occurrences in all celestial bodies, not just the earth. The *weather forecaster*, often called the *weatherman*, is probably the most popular of the several different types of meteorologists.

Women represented approximately 2 per cent of the somewhat fewer than 5,000 meteorologists at work in the United States in 1970. The majority of them were employed by agencies of the federal government.

Oceanographers study and investigate the characteristics, movement, physical properties and plant and animal life of the oceans. To explore the oceans, oceanographers use miscellaneous probing instruments, special cameras for underwater use and sensitive sounding devices. In 1970, it was estimated that there were approximately 6,000 oceanographers at work in the United States; the number of female oceanographers was so small that their percentage was not even computed. The majority worked for the federal government, colleges and universities.

The minimum educational requirement for entry into any of the environmental sciences is a bachelor's degree with major in the specific science of your choice. To attain professional status in geology, geophysics, meteorology or oceanography, a master's degree is necessary; for those who wish to advance, do research or teach on the college or university level, a doctor's degree in the respective specialty is generally desirable.

Environmental scientists often work outdoors, and the work may require much physical stamina. Curiosity about planet earth and other celestial bodies, an analytical mind and scientific interest and ability are necessary for success in these fields. The employment outlook in the environmental sciences is favorable for those with graduate degrees.

Girls, if you are enchanted by the earth and the water, air and space around it, give thought to the environmental sciences, for here, where women rarely tread, the doors have begun to open to admit you. If you acquire advanced degrees in the field of your interest, you should find bright prospects for future employment; as a matter of fact, in view of present trends, you may find the doors wider open to you than to young men with similar training.

For additional information about careers in these fields, write to one or more of the following professional associations according to your individual interests:

American Geological Institute
2201 M St. N.W.
Washington, D.C. 20037

American Geophysical Union
1707 L St. N.W.
Washington, D.C. 20036

American Meteorological Society
45 Beacon Street
Boston, Mass. 02108

American Society for Oceanography
Department of the Marine Technology Society
1730 M St. N.W.
Washington, D.C. 20036

NONTRADITIONAL CAREERS FOR WOMEN

There are many varieties of *life scientists,* but they all have in common their concern with living organisms. They study the way plants, animals and microbes live, grow and undergo changes. Those life scientists whose work is of a general nature, covering more than one of the broad areas of this field, are known as *biologists* or *biological scientists.*

Based on the type of organisms on which they concentrate their work activities, life scientists are classified as *botanists, zoologists* or *microbiologists.*

Botanists study plants. Many of them specialize in a particular aspect of plant life. *Plant ecologists* study the effects of rain, sunlight, temperature and other environmental elements on the distribution and type of plant growth. *Plant morphologists* investigate the structure of plants and plant cells. *Plant pathologists* are concerned with the cause and control of diseases of plants. *Plant physiologists* study the life processes, such as growth, development and reproduction, of plants. *Plant taxonomists* identify and classify plants.

Zoologists study animals. Those who specialize in certain types of animals have titles identifying the kind of animal life they study. Thus, *herpetologists* study reptiles and amphibians, *ichthyologists* study fishes, *mammalogists* study mammals and *ornithologists* study birds.

The terms "microbiology" and "bacteriology," until recently, were used interchangeably. *Microbiology* and *microbiologist* are now preferred to *bacteriology* and *bacteriologist* because the former terms are more all-inclusive. *Microbiologists* investigate all forms of microorganisms, including bacteria, molds, viruses and other microscopic and submicroscopic organisms. *Bacteriologists* study bacteria. *Virologists* specialize in the study of viruses.

The American Society for Microbiology had a membership of more than 15,000 in 1972. Of this number, 24.5 per cent (approximately 3,800) were women; this was an increase over pre-

112

Women in Math and Science

ceding years. In April, 1970, the Committee on the Status of Women Microbiologists of the American Society of Microbiology was formed "to investigate the present situation regarding the status of women members, and to make recommendations and actively work with institutions and departments to ensure full and equal opportunity for educational, career and personal development for all microbiologists."

In addition to the grouping of life scientists as botanists, zoologists and microbiologists, they are also classified according to the nature of their work and the approaches they use; the life scientists in this system of classification may be found to overlap in any one, two or all three of the botany, zoology or microbiology groups. On this basis, there are many varieties of life scientists, including *agronomists, anatomists, biochemists, biological oceanographers, biophysicists, ecologists, embryologists, entomologists, geneticists, horticulturists, husbandry specialists, nutritionists, pathologists, pharmacologists* and *physiologists.*

Agronomists conduct investigations and experiments aimed at improving crops and the soil. They develop new methods of growing crops in order to obtain more efficient production, higher yield and improved quality of the crops.

Anatomists are concerned with the form and structure of different organisms. They conduct examinations by observation and dissection, sometimes with the aid of microscopes, depending upon the size of what they are examining. They may specialize in the structure of plant and animal cells and are then known as *cytologists,* or in the structure of tissues and organs, in which case they are known as *histologists.*

Biochemists combine a knowledge of biology and chemistry to investigate the chemical composition of living organisms. They analyze the chemical processes related to biological functions and examine the effects of foods, drugs, hormones and other substances on the tissues and vital functions of living things. To examine the problems of discrimination against women in

113

this field, the American Society of Biological Chemists formed the Committee on Women in Biochemistry in 1972.

Biological oceanographers are also called *aquatic biologists.* They study plants and animals living in the oceans and other bodies of water and investigate the environmental conditions affecting them.

Biophysicists are knowledgeable about both biology and physics. They investigate the physical principles of living cells and organisms. They study the electrical and mechanical energy of these living things and the interrelationships of biological functions and physical forces, such as heat, light, radiation and sound.

Ecologists study the relationships between organisms and their environment. They are concerned about the effects of the air, rainfall, temperature and other environmental influences on the biological functions of plants and animals. They may specialize and, depending upon their specialty, be either *animal ecologists* or *plant ecologists.* The latter are defined in the earlier section on botanists.

Embryologists investigate the development of an organism from the fertilized egg to the formation of the complete organism. They explore the how and why of this development and seek the causes and means of preventing abnormalities that may occur during the processes of development.

Entomologists study insects and their relation to plant and animal life. They are interested in controlling and eliminating harmful insects and in encouraging the growth of beneficial insects, such as bees. Those who specialize in bee culture and breeding are known as *apiculturists.*

Foresters are professionals who combine a knowledge of conservation and the life sciences. They are concerned about the protection of our nation's forests and their resources. They manage, develop and protect the timber, water, wildlife, forage and recreation areas. In 1972, the Society of American Foresters had about 18,000 members, of whom a mere sixty-four were women; but it is significant that most of these women became members since 1968. Would you like to be a forester? If you would, then go ahead; major in forestry at college and have no fear about entering this formerly all-male profession.

Geneticists study heredity and investigate the origin, transmission and development of inherited traits. Some are concerned primarily about breeding desirable characteristics and thus improving plant and animal breeds and are known accordingly as *plant breeders* and *animal breeders*.

Horticulture involves the cultivation of flowers, fruits, ornamental plants and vegetables. *Horticulturists* strive to improve the methods of growing, harvesting, storing and transporting horticultural crops. They conduct experiments to develop new or improved varieties of fruits, nuts, berries, vegetables, flowers, bushes and trees. Horticulturists who specialize in flowers, ornamental plants and trees are called *floriculturists;* those who specialize in vegetables are *olericulturists,* and those who specialize in fruits, nuts and berries are *pomologists.*

Husbandry specialists perform experiments relating to the selection, breeding, feeding, management and marketing of beef and dual-purpose cattle, sheep, hogs, goats and other domestic farm animals. *Animal husbandmen, dog breeders* and *cattle ranchers* do research to develop better practices in sanitation, housing and parasite and disease control to improve the health and yield of these animals.

Nutritionists examine foods to determine the percentages of essential ingredients contained in them. They are concerned with the kinds and amounts of food elements needed to build and repair body tissues and maintain health. They study how these food elements, such as fats, minerals, proteins, sugars and vitamins, are changed into body substances and energy.

Pharmacologists study the effects of drugs and other substances on the tissues of animals and human beings. They perform ex-

115

periments with animals to study the effects of these substances on the circulation of the blood, respiration (breathing), digestion and other vital functions of these animals. They standardize the procedures for manufacturing miscellaneous drugs and medicinal compounds and may develop new chemical compounds for use in drugs and medicines.

Physiologists are concerned with the functions and structure of cells, tissues and organs. They study biological activities and functions, such as circulation, excretion, respiration and reproduction, under normal and abnormal conditions. They may specialize in the study of a particular body area or system, such as the digestive, circulatory or nervous system.

There is so much to the science of life. Living things are fascinating. You may work outdoors or in, with large animals or viruses, pore over microscopes or pour solutions into test tubes; but whatever you do as a life scientist, you should be propelled by a curiosity about living things and have scientific interest and ability to excel in scientific subjects. Whether you are interested in leaves or puppies, microbes or guppies, cows or pharmacology, flowers or physiology, if you delight in the study of living things, you should be able to find a place for yourself in any one of many life science careers.

Your special interests may steer you toward a particular pathway in this vast field. Regardless of the kind of life scientist you choose to become, you will need to complete four years of college and obtain your undergraduate degree in a broad base of the life sciences, including courses in a number of the other sciences.

If you wish to advance beyond the beginner's position, you must do graduate work in the particular area of your interest and obtain a master's degree. Those who would like to do advanced research or teach on the college or university level should continue their graduate studies to the completion of their Ph.D. degree with special concentration in the selected aspect of the life sciences which interests them most.

Unfortunately, as in many of the professions and other occupations, exact figures on the number of women employed in the life sciences are not available. It can only be estimated that women represent about 10 per cent of the total number of life scientists; there are about 180,000 life scientists employed throughout the United States, with the largest numbers working in colleges, universities, medical schools, hospitals and government agencies. Microbiology seems to attract more women than any other area of the life sciences; almost one-fourth of the membership of the American Society of Microbiology in 1972 were women.

A rapid increase in employment opportunities is anticipated in the life sciences throughout the 1970s. Women are needed in this field. Get the best possible education and training in your chosen area of interest, and you will find there is a welcome mat for qualified women in the life sciences.

For more details about careers in the life sciences, write to one or more of the following depending upon your individual interests:

American Institute of Biological Sciences
3900 Wisconsin Ave. N.W.
Washington, D.C. 20016

American Physiological Society
9650 Rockville Pike
Bethesda, Md. 20014

American Society for Microbiology
1913 I St. N.W.
Washington, D.C. 20006

American Society for Microbiology
Committee on the Status of Women Microbiologists
Dr. Mary Louise Robbins, Chairman
George Washington University
School of Medicine
1339 H St. N.W.
Washington, D.C. 20005

American Society of Biological Chemists
9650 Rockville Pike
Bethesda, Md. 20014

American Society of Biological Chemists
Committee on Women in Biochemistry
Dr. Loretta Leive, Chairperson
U.S. Public Health Service
National Institutes of Health
Building 4, Room 116
Bethesda, Md. 10014.

American Society of Horticultural Science
615 Elm Street
St. Joseph, Mich. 49085

Society of American Foresters
1010 16th St. N.W.
Washington, D.C. 20036

The *physical scientists* are involved in work activities concerned with the basic laws of the physical world. Among the natural sciences, they constitute the largest field of employment. In 1970, there were approximately 250,000 physical scientists at work in the United States. They include the *astronomers, chemists, food scientists* and *physicists*.

The largest of the physical science specialties is chemistry. There were about 137,000 *chemists* at work in 1970. Next came about 50,000 *physicists*, more than 7,000 *food scientists* and approximately 1,400 *astronomers;* the remainder belonged to many miscellaneous minor specialties categorized within the large scope of the physical sciences.

Chemistry and the work done by *chemists* affect much of our daily lives. The antibiotics which help to make you well again when you are ill, the detergents you use to clean your clothes, the frozen foods you eat, the odor-free paints which beautify your walls, the polyesters you wear, the plastics which serve you in so many ways—all of these and much more are the products of modern chemistry.

Chemists conduct all sorts of chemical tests and experiments; they do analyses of a qualitative and quantitative nature.

Industrial chemists do analytical and research chemical work in an industrial setting; some work in such industrial fields as dyes, paints, pharmaceuticals, plastics and resins.

Inorganic chemists perform experiments on substances which are free or relatively free of carbons; they develop and improve inorganic products and materials. *Organic chemists* do experiments on substances of which carbon is the essential element and strive to develop and improve organic products and materials.

Research chemists conduct investigations and perform experiments, using their specialized knowledge of chemistry, to develop new products and new processes, or they do research in which they apply their knowledge of chemical techniques and methods to solve technical problems.

Entry positions in this field require a minimum of the bachelor's degree with a major in chemistry. Promotion to higher status generally calls for graduate training leading to a master's degree in chemistry. The Ph.D. degree is desirable for advancement to top-level research and administrative positions.

Do you like to work with your hands and do experiments? Do you find your science and math courses fascinating? Do chemicals intrigue you? If your answers are "Yes" and you are persevering, inquisitive, able to concentrate on detail, capable of preparing well-written reports on the experiments conducted and have a good memory, then a career in chemistry may be for you.

Chemists are found in many different types of laboratories, and their work activities are very varied. Some help to develop new vaccines and antibodies; others do research on insecticides, ny-

119

lons, plastics, synthetic rubber and rocket fuel; and others yet are concerned about bulk properties rather than individual molecules of matter.

Of the 137,000 chemists at work in this country in 1970, about 7 per cent were women. The same percentage was found in the membership of the American Chemical Society; A.C.S. had approximately 100,000 members, of whom about 7,000 were women. About 75 per cent of these chemists were employed by private industry; most of the remainder worked for colleges and universities, research organizations, government agencies and health institutions.

In 1970, 15.7 per cent of the 7,794 bachelor's degrees in chemistry were granted to women; 22.7 per cent of the 1,665 master's degrees and 8 per cent of the 2,145 Ph.D. degrees in chemistry were awarded to women. Thus, the percentage of women in chemistry is on its way up beyond the 7 per cent figure.

The long-range employment outlook for chemists is favorable. It is anticipated that by 1980 there will be a demand for 200,000 chemists, an increase of approximately 50 per cent over the number of chemists employed in 1972; much of this will be the result of increasing production of drugs, fertilizers, man-made fibers, plastics and high-energy and nuclear fuels.

Over 60 per cent of the women members of the American Chemical Society in 1972 had at least the master's degree in chemistry; over 30 per cent had earned their Ph.D. degree. The positions at which they were employed ranged from the technician level all the way up to full professors of chemistry in colleges and universities and top-level managerial posts in industry and government.

In 1927, female members of the American Chemical Society formed the Women's Service Committee. In September, 1971, to better define the role of this committee, its name was officially changed to the Women Chemists Committee. Among the objectives of this committee are "to serve as a forum for the problems of women in chemistry, to develop concrete recommendations regarding these problems and solutions, to provide a means of increasing and improving participation of women chemists in the society." This committee consists of fifteen A.C.S. members who represent different geographic areas and different employment settings (industry, government and colleges and universities).

The Chairman of the Women Chemists Committee is Helen M. Free, who has had a most interesting career in this field. She says, "I started my college career with the full intention of becoming an 'old-maid Latin teacher'—a far cry from a married industrial chemist with half-a-dozen offspring!"

"I changed my major to chemistry the semester after Pearl Harbor," she explains, "when all the science departments were actively recruiting females. I've never regretted the switch and would recommend a chemistry major to all gals who think they'd like it. After I was graduated from the College of Wooster (Wooster, Ohio) with honors in chemistry, I applied for a position as a control chemist at Miles Laboratories, and for several research assistantships. It was only after I had accepted the offer from Miles that the research assistantships began to come through. I felt disappointed at the time not to be able to accept the more glamorous-type jobs—but I'm not sorry I've worked in industry, for I've had an interesting and varied career in the Miles-Ames complex of laboratories in such areas as research, applied product development, technical services, teaching and finally in the growth and development department of Ames Company in my present position as New Products Manager for Clinical Test Systems."

Helen M. Free continues: "During my third year at Miles Laboratories, I just happened to marry the boss, and Al and I worked together as a scientific team for many years. Many of the basic concepts and much of my philosophy in regard to research, biochemistry, clinical chemistry, careers for women and the business world in general, I learned from him. My advice

121

for a woman who is considering a career and family as a double lifetime job is to first find an *actively* understanding husband such as mine. An actively understanding husband is one who will consider his wife's career as important to her and the family as his is to him and the family."

"Each partner," she adds, "must build a meaningful relationship into both careers and both must contribute to the total family picture. Both my husband and I have presented literally hundreds of papers at scientific meetings all over the world. We've always taken the children to scientific meetings, and so they're all seasoned travelers. A gal *can* combine a career and family and she *can* be a success at both, but she has to work harder—to prove to her co-workers and to herself that it *can* be done."

"I do not recommend," emphasizes this accomplished chemist, "that every woman have a career outside the home and I object to having other women tell me I should 'stay at home with the children.' We should each 'do our own thing' and make sure the 'own thing' we choose is fun for us. Above all, a gal should not feel guilty about the choice she makes, but should enjoy the rewards as they come. Rewards (professional and as a family member) I've had include the introduction of a new product to the clinical laboratory after traumatic years of development and seeing my oldest son as a successful teacher in his hometown; the good feeling from the expanding sales of my world-wide company and the all-'A's report card of my next-youngest daughter; the thrill of being corecipient, with my husband, of the Honor Scroll Award of the Chicago American Institute of Chemists and the anniversary card to the 'peanut butter and jelly of parents.'"

Those of you who would like additional information about careers in chemistry should write to either or both of the following: American Chemical Society, 1155 16 St. N.W., Washington, D.C. 20036, and/or Helen M. Free, Chairman, Women Chemists

Committee of A.C.S., c/o Ames Company, Division of Miles Laboratories, 1127 Myrtle Street, Elkhart, Ind. 46514.

Physics has long been considered a "male-only" field. In 1970, women represented only about 4 per cent of the employed physicists in this country; there were then fewer than 2,000 women physicists in the United States. Opportunities for women in physics are better today, however, than they ever were before.

Physicists conduct experiments with betatrons, cyclotrons, electron microscopes, lasers, spectrometers, telescopes and other instruments and equipment to observe the structure and properties of matter, the transformation and propagation of energy, the relationships between matter and energy and other physical phenomena. They observe, analyze and describe the behavior of the forces at work in the physical world. Electromagnetism, gravity, heat flow and radioactivity are among their concerns. Modern progress in such areas as aerospace, communications, electronics and nuclear energy is the result of the contributions physicists have made to our store of scientific knowledge.

Acoustic physicists study and research the phenomena of hearing, sound reproduction and vibration. They devise acoustical systems and design amplifiers, loudspeakers, recorders and other equipment employed in sound reproduction.

Atomic and molecular physicists conduct research into the structure and behavior of atoms and molecules, except nuclei, and perform experiments in the practical applications of atomic and molecular physics in industrial, military and other fields.

Nuclear physicists study and investigate the nature and characteristics of atomic nuclei. They may specialize in such areas as nuclear spectroscopy, radioactive isotopes, cosmic radiation or nuclear theory.

Do you wonder how that television picture got into your TV tube? Are you fascinated by each space shot? Have you wondered why what goes up comes down again? Do you marvel at the accomplishments of the tiny transistor? Are you consumed by scientific curiosity? Do you have mechanical ability, manual dexterity and scientific aptitude? If your answers to these questions are "Yes" and you excel in science and math, then a career in physics may be attractive to you and appropriate for you.

If you want to become a physicist, if energy and matter and physical phenomena intrigue you, don't let anyone discourage you. To achieve professional status as a physicist, after obtaining your bachelor's degree with a major in physics, you will need to continue on into graduate school for your master's degree. This will qualify you for many research positions in private industry, research institutes, colleges and universities and government agencies.

The Ph.D. degree in some specialized area of physics is required for higher-level positions in research and development projects and for professorial status at colleges and universities.

The long-range employment outlook for physicists is very favorable for females with advanced degrees. It is anticipated that by 1980 the demand for physicists will reach 75,000; this represents an increase of about 50 per cent above the number of physicists at work in 1972. Qualified female physicists should find many and varied opportunities available to them, especially in complex research and development positions.

The American Physical Society, in April, 1971, created the Committee on Women in Physics "to study the situation of women physicists and to make recommendations based on this study." Among the many results of this study, it was found that women physicists enjoy their work and are successful in surmounting the difficulties they may encounter. It was also found that 60 per cent of all the women and 75 per cent of the "Ph.D. women" who replied to the "working group" questionnaires are married; 74 per cent of these married women are mothers and have an average of 1.9 children, showing that a career in physics and marriage and motherhood do mix well.

124

In 1972, this committee's name was changed to Committee on the Status of Women in Physics. Among its many aims are to assist women physicists with special employment problems and to study the changing situation with regard to women physicists. For additional information about careers in physics, write to Dr. Elizabeth Baranger, Committee on the Status of Women in Physics, Room 6-405, Massachusetts Institute of Technology, Cambridge, Mass. 02139, and/or the American Physical Society (a member society of the American Institute of Physics), 335 East 45th Street, New York, N.Y. 10017.

Astronomers form one of the smallest groups of physical scientists; their work centers on the structure, extent and evolution of the universe. In 1972, the American Astronomical Society had a total membership of 2,800, of whom about 200 were women.

Astronomers use telescopes to which special photographic and other optical devices are attached to enable them to observe and interpret celestial phenomena. They collect and analyze information on the positions and other aspects of the sun, moons, planets, stars, nebulae and galaxies. They make all sorts of astronomical observations for theoretical purposes and practical applications.

Since the field of astronomy is such a small one, the number of employment opportunities for males as well as females is limited, but positions are available equally to all on the basis of professional qualifications. If you are spellbound by the heavens and the stars and all else that constitute the universe and believe that astronomy is the career for you, then after your graduation from college with a science major continue on with your graduate studies until the completion of your Ph.D. in astronomy. About 75 per cent of all astronomers work in colleges and universities, many in university-operated observatories, and others for federal government agencies.

Further details about careers in astronomy may be had from the American Astronomical Society, 211 FitzRandolph Road, Princeton, N.J. 08540.

Another group of professionals classed within the category of physical scientists consists of the *food scientists*. Within this group are a miscellany of scientists who investigate the basic physical, chemical and biological nature of food.

Food scientists are also known as *food technologists*. The Institute of Food Technologists, in 1972, had approximately 11,000 members, of whom it was estimated that about 15 to 20 per cent were women. Food scientists are concerned with the processing, preserving and storing of an adequate, nutritious and wholesome food supply. They may develop new food products, test new additives for purity, investigate changes occurring during processing and perform varied other research, development and quality-control tests.

To obtain a beginning position as a food scientist, you will need a bachelor's degree with a major in food science or one of the physical or life sciences. A master's degree is essential if you would like to advance and do research in food science.

Women have excellent opportunities in this field. The outlook for female food scientists is favorable for the years ahead, largely because of the increasing demands for a greater variety of high-quality processed foods. Often women who start out toward careers as dietitians, nutritionists or home economists modify their objectives and become food scientists.

Additional career information in this field may be obtained by writing to the Institute of Food Technologists, 221 N. LaSalle St., Suite 2120, Chicago, Ill. 60601.

At the Council meeting of the American Association for the Advancement of Science on December 30, 1971, the following resolution was adopted on behalf of the A.A.A.S. Women's Caucus: "Whereas the talents and contributions of women in science are not fully recognized and utilized, whereas there is no central listing of women in science, be it resolved that the Council and Board of the American Association for the Advancement of Science immediately establish an Office for Women's

Equality to work toward full representation and opportunity for women in scientific training and employment, affairs of the association, and in the direction of national science policy." For further information, write to the Women's Caucus, American Association for the Advancement of Science, 1515 Massachusetts Ave. N.W., Washington, D.C. 20005.

At the 1971 meeting of the Federation of American Societies for Experimental Biology, a group of women scientists founded the Association of Women in Science "to promote equal opportunities for women to enter the professions and to achieve their career goals." Membership in A.W.I.S. is open to women in all of the scientific fields. Further information about A.W.I.S. may be obtained from Dr. Estelle R. Ramey, President, Association of Women in Science, Inc., Georgetown University, School of Medicine, Department of Physiology and Biophysics, Washington, D.C. 20007.

Chapter 7

ENGINEERING WOMEN HAVE FAST-GROWING FUTURES

THERE are those who have aptitude and interest in science and math, but prefer to seek a career essentially in mathematics, such as mathematician or statistician, while others with the same abilities and interests prefer a career that is essentially scientific in nature, such as botanist or geologist.

There also are those who would like a career that combines their aptitude and interest in both science and math. The field of engineering does this and it offers women tens of thousands of such career opportunities annually. It is true that in most science careers competency and interest in mathematics are necessary. However, in no other careers are ability in both science and math as necessary as in engineering.

Ah, but be prepared! If you should tell your relatives or friends that you are giving thought to becoming an engineer, surely there will be those among them who will laugh at you and say, "You can't become an engineer, you're a girl!"

Well, you laugh right back at them and tell them to awake and enter today's world.

It is true that of all the professions, engineering has the tiniest percentage of female members. In 1970, there were about 1,100,000 engineers at work in the United States, and only approximately 8,000 (less than 1 per cent) were women. This severe sexist discrimination came about *not* because men are qualified to be engineers and women are not, but because girls in high school and college were brainwashed into believing that engineering is a field for males only. Females have been discouraged from becoming engineers, whereas males have been encouraged to do so.

Of course, there are those who will persist in telling you that females do not have what it takes to be engineers. Well, this is definitely not so. Actually, in a study of eleventh-grade students conducted by the U.S. Department of Labor, it was found that two-thirds as many girls as boys have engineering aptitude. This means that for every three boys with engineering aptitude, there are two girls similarly endowed! This is a far cry from the meager "less than 1 per cent" present female representation in the engineering profession.

The barriers of discrimination and discouragement are giving way, girls, and tremendous opportunities await you in the engineering profession. Are you superior in math and science? Can you visualize size, form and function? Are you curious about why and how certain things take place? Do you approach problems in a logical manner? Would you like to develop and design new products and/or devise ways and means to improve an existing product and make it cheaper too? If your replies are "Yes," then you should certainly give consideration to a career in engineering.

Engineers are of many different types depending upon the branch of engineering in which they work. Actually the term "engineer" is an all-encompassing one applied to persons who possess the required qualifications, training, work experience and certification to perform professional functions in any one or more branches of engineering.

Engineers apply scientific principles to solve problems in designing goods and services and in developing methods for the production of these goods and services. The basic difference between the engineer and the scientist is that the engineer applies scientific principles, whereas the scientist concentrates on the discovery of such principles. The engineer's major work activities center on design, development, research and testing.

Engineers apply mathematics, science and technology to improve just about every aspect of our way of living. Almost every industry you can imagine comes within the range of engineers' activities. Washing machines, television sets, air conditioners, bridges, highways, heating systems, fabrics, detergents, air pollution control, mass transit, urban renewal, our national defense system—all of these are among the many concerns included within the vast scope of engineering.

The six largest branches of engineering are (1) electrical, (2) mechanical, (3) civil, (4) industrial, (5) aerospace and (6) chemical.

In 1970, there were more than 235,000 *electrical engineers* at work throughout the country. Electrical engineers, including *electronics engineers,* constitute the largest group of engineers. Their work centers on the design and development of electrical and electronic equipment. Included among the latter are miscellaneous equipment ranging all the way from the latest satellite communications systems to electronic computers, missile and spacecraft guidance and transmitting instruments, navigational equipment, radar, sonar, telephony, television and even that tiny transistor radio in your pocket. These engineers are involved, too, in the design of facilities for generating and distributing electric power.

Mechanical engineers in 1970 numbered about 220,000. They design and develop a variety of machines, including power-producing machines, such as internal combustion engines, steam and gas turbines, jet and rocket engines and nuclear reactors, and machines which use power, such as refrigeration and air-conditioning equipment, elevators, machine tools, printing presses and steel rolling mills.

130

Engineering Women Have Fast-Growing Futures

About 185,000 *civil engineers* were at work in the United States in 1970. The work of civil engineers involves the design, planning and supervision of the construction of airfields, bridges, dams, harbors, highways, railroads, tunnels, viaducts, water supply and sewage systems and other structures.

Industrial engineers numbered approximately 125,000 in 1970. These engineers are concerned with the most efficient use of manpower, materials and machines in the processes of mass production.

There were over 65,000 *aerospace engineers* employed in the United States in 1970. They play a dominant role in our space program. Aerospace engineers design and develop a variety of aircraft structures, conventional aircraft, guided missiles, helicopters, propulsion systems, rockets, spacecraft and supersonic transports.

Approximately 50,000 *chemical engineers* were at work in this country in 1970. They design plants and equipment involved in the manufacture of chemicals and chemical products and are concerned with the development of the most efficient manufacturing processes of these products.

There are more than twenty-five branches of engineering and many of these specialties have subbranches. For example, among the civil engineers, there are the *highway engineers* who specialize in the design and development of highways. Women engineers, although they represent such a minuscule percentage of the total number of engineers, are nonetheless found, albeit in only a tiny number in some cases, in all of these branches of engineering. In 1972, the Society of Women Engineers conducted a survey of women engineers. A good deal of similarity was found between the branches of engineering in which the women specialized and those in which the men specialized.

Like the male engineers, the largest number of female engineers were in electrical (including electronics) engineering. The second largest number of female engineers was found to be in

131

NONTRADITIONAL CAREERS FOR WOMEN

aerospace engineering, which ranks in fifth place in popularity among male engineers. Tied for third place among the women was mechanical engineering, which ranks second among the men, and computer engineering. *Computer engineers* set up and operate computers to solve scientific and engineering problems; they formulate mathematical models of these problems and develop new techniques for solving problems. Civil engineering and chemical engineering were tied for next place among women engineers; among the men, these two specialties rank in third and sixth place respectively. A handful of women are members of the specialty of industrial engineering, which is the fourth most popular male specialty.

Some female engineers are found too in the specialties of agricultural, biomedical, ceramic, metallurgical, mining and nuclear engineering. *Agricultural engineers* are concerned with the design and development of equipment, machinery and methods to build up the economy and efficiency of the production, processing and distribution of food and other agricultural products. *Biomedical engineers* apply engineering technology and knowledge of medical and biological sciences to solve medical and health-related problems.

Ceramic engineers design machinery and develop techniques for processing clay, silicates and other nonmetallic minerals into a vast variety of ceramic products. *Metallurgical engineers* are involved with the processing of metals and the conversion of these metals into finished, useful products.

Mining engineers determine the location and plan the extraction of coal, metallic ores, nonmetallic minerals and building materials, such as stone or gravel from the earth, and then prepare these for use by manufacturing industries. *Nuclear engineers* apply the principles and theory of nuclear science to problems involving the control, release and utilization of nuclear energy and perform design and development work in which the major challenge is the unique nature of nuclear energy.

132

Engineering Women Have Fast-Growing Futures

To enter the field of engineering, whether you decide to become a general engineer or specialize in any one of the branches or subbranches, you should get your bachelor's degree in engineering. There are approximately 270 colleges, universities and engineering schools offering this degree; some have four-year and others have five-year curricula.

Check with the schools you might like to attend to determine the length and nature of their individual programs of study; there are some that require the students to take liberal arts courses for three years and engineering courses for two years and award a bachelor's degree in liberal arts and in engineering to those students who successfully complete the combined five years of study.

For advancement, especially into higher-level research positions, graduate degrees are often desirable. There are some specialties—for example, nuclear engineering—for which undergraduate training is not available. You must continue on into graduate level if you wish to enter these specialties.

Engineers who offer their services to the public or whose work activities may affect life, health or property are required to be licensed. All of the fifty states and the District of Columbia call for such licensing, and generally the candidates for a license must be graduates of an accredited engineering curriculum, have at least four years of experience and pass a state licensing examination.

Only teaching has more members in its profession than engineering, which makes engineering the second largest profession. Of the almost 1,100,000 engineers at work in the United States, about 60 per cent are employed in the manufacturing industries, particularly aircraft and parts, chemicals, electrical equipment, fabricated metal products, instruments, machinery and motor vehicles industries. The remainder may be found in the construction field, public utilities, consulting services, government agencies, colleges and universities and research organizations.

NONTRADITIONAL CAREERS FOR WOMEN

The survey conducted by the Society of Women Engineers, mentioned earlier in this chapter, found that no one industry plays a major role as an employer of women engineers. The largest percentage of women engineers was employed in aircraft and space industries, although these industries employed only 12 per cent of the respondents to this survey. Next, in the following order, came electronic equipment and services, computers, educational and information services, construction and civil engineering, communication, machinery and mechanical equipment, electrical equipment and services, utilities, transportation, petroleum, metal fabricated products, motor vehicles, ceramics, agriculture, ordnance and miscellaneous other areas (not identified), each with less than 1 per cent of the respondents to this survey.

Of the women who responded to this survey, 55 per cent were married, 34 per cent were single, 7 per cent were divorced and 4 per cent were widowed. Thirty-eight per cent of these women engineers indicated that they have children; of these, 30 per cent stated that they have one child, 34 per cent two children, 22 per cent three children, 8 per cent four children and 6 per cent five or more children. Thus, marriage and motherhood are obviously quite compatible with an engineering career.

The Society of Women Engineers was founded in 1949-50. Small groups of women engineers had begun to meet in New York, Boston, Philadelphia and Washington, D.C. As a result, the Society of Women Engineers was incorporated in 1952. In 1961, it established its headquarters in the United Engineering Center in New York City. Today S.W.E. is the professional organization of women engineers. It aims to encourage women engineers to high levels of achievement and to encourage young women to consider a career in engineering.

Naomi J. McAfee is the President of the Society of Women Engineers. She says, "As a small child, I had dreams of becoming a great scientist. As I grew up and went to college, I found that physics was the area of study which I liked the best. In August of 1956, I was graduated with a B.S. degree in Physics from Western Kentucky State College, and my first job was with Westinghouse Electric Corporation in Baltimore. I worked as an engineer in their Reliability Engineering Section. My entry into engineering was accidental, but has been very rewarding. Through the years, it has become increasingly obvious to me that my forte is working with the development of hardware rather than being an experimentalist in some laboratory. Perhaps there are those that would argue that what I'm doing is only an extension of physics, and I'll agree, but it is also engineering."

"I've only worked with this one company," she adds. "Several of my male counterparts think that one should change jobs every two or three years. Perhaps so, but it can be done within the company as well as moving outside. My career growth has been faster than most of the men and I attribute that to being dependable—i.e., staying with the company."

"I've held several positions with Westinghouse," continues President McAfee. "I started as an engineer, moved to become a group leader, was then promoted to fellow engineer, was promoted to supervisory engineer (the first woman in the corporation to hold this title), then promoted to manager, reliability, maintainability and safety engineering and, finally, to my present position as Manager, Quality and Reliability Assurance. I have encountered very little discrimination in my career, and I feel that one has to prove oneself regardless. Being a woman made things a little slower as far as getting into management, but up until my last assignment, my rate of progress as far as promotions and salary were concerned has been greater than that of men in comparable positions."

"My current job," she says, "includes direct supervision of ten managers who have 115 engineers working for them and coordination of six departments and five divisions with over 13,000 employees. As Manager, Quality and Reliability Assurance, for the Westinghouse Electric Corporation's Defense and Electronic Systems Center in Baltimore, my responsibilities include directing all of the engineering department's reliability, maintainability and safety engineering activities in support of the center's development, equipment design and production programs. It also includes planning, organizing, implementing and controlling all functions of quality on all programs as well as directing the activities of the Failure Analysis Laboratory, Data Center and the Semiconductor Analysis Laboratory of the Applied Technology Laboratory. The responsibilities include the development of new concepts and techniques, selection and training of personnel, establishing budgets, controlling expenditures and maintaining schedules."

"Engineering is a dynamic career," President McAfee says. "Technology today is changing more rapidly than it has at any time in history. Yet technology is the answer to all of our problems associated with pollution, ecology and maintaining the current standard of living. I would recommend that any woman who is interested in mathematics or the related physical sciences consider engineering as a career. The demand for trained engineers in all fields is increasing, while the supply of graduate engineers decreases every year. The need for intelligent people who are capable of making decisions is here. The rewards are tremendous and the pay is great."

As Naomi J. McAfee says, there is a great need for women engineers. Women could bring to engineering their special interests in the conservation of our natural resources, the production and maintenance of a high-quality environment and the control and prevention of pollution, all of which are among our many contemporary engineering problems. Environmental control and ecological problems particularly will create an increasing demand for the services of engineers.

The long-range outlook for employment of engineers is very favorable. Interestingly, the employment outlook appears to be even better for females than for males; in specialty after specialty of engineering, it is stated that young women engineers are in greater demand than young male engineers.

Thirty-one per cent of the engineers in the U.S.S.R. are women, while here in the United States the figure is woefully less than 1 per cent. Women are needed in our country to aid in our continuing technological advancement. Some girls are frightened away from engineering careers by being told that most of the work is done outdoors and is physically demanding. This is definitely not so. The nature of engineering work has changed a great deal in recent years. A large proportion of the work consists of designing, estimating and planning, most of which is done indoors in pleasant, well-ventilated offices.

If you have interest and aptitude in math and science, an analytical mind, a capacity for detail, the ability to communicate your ideas and the zest for solving problems, then give serious thought to a career in engineering, for much challenge and satisfaction await you in this profession.

For further information about engineering careers for women, write to the Society of Women Engineers, United Engineering Center, 345 East 47th St., New York, N.Y. 10017, and/or the Committee on Professional Opportunities for Women, Institute of Electrical and Electronics Engineers, 345 East 47th St., New York, N.Y. 10017.

Additionally, depending upon your individual interests, write to any one or more of the following for information about engineering careers, schools and licensing:

Engineers' Council for Professional Development
345 East 47th Street
New York, N.Y. 10017

National Society of Professional Engineers
2029 K St. N.W.
Washington, D.C. 20006

American Institute of Aeronautics and Astronautics
1290 Avenue of the Americas
New York, N.Y. 10019

American Society of Agricultural Engineers
2950 Niles Road
St. Joseph, Mich. 49085

Biomedical Engineering Society
P. O. Box 1600
Evanston, Ind. 60204

American Ceramic Society
4055 N. High Street
Columbus, Ohio 43214

American Institute of Chemical Engineers
345 East 47th Street
New York, N.Y. 10017

American Society of Civil Engineers
345 East 47th Street
New York, N.Y. 10017

Institute of Electrical and Electronics Engineers
345 East 47th Street
New York, N.Y. 10017

American Institute of Industrial Engineers
25 Technology Park/Atlanta
Norcross, Ga. 30071

American Society of Mechanical Engineers
345 East 47th Street
New York, N.Y. 10017

American Institute of Mining, Metallurgical and Petroleum
  Engineers
345 East 47th Street
New York, N.Y. 10017

Engineering Women Have Fast-Growing Futures

Perhaps you do not wish to be either a scientist, mathematician or engineer, but you would like to work with these people. You can do this by becoming a technician. Science and technology have made great strides since the end of World War II. This technological progress was made possible to a large measure by the activities of *engineering and science technicians.* These technicians are practical middlemen between the engineers and scientists, on the one hand, and the skilled craftspeople on the production line (see Chapter 10), on the other.

The exact number of women technicians is unknown. However, it has been estimated that women represent about 11 per cent of the total number of technicians. In 1970, there were almost 1,000,000 technicians (engineering and science technicians and draftsmen) employed in the United States.

Draftswomen and *draftsmen* are usually classed within the category of technicians. Although among all technicians, women represent about 11 per cent of the total number, draftswomen represent only about 4 per cent of their group. Draftswomen draw up plans that indicate the exact physical dimensions and specifications of the objects and products conceived by engineers, designers and architects.

Engineering and science technicians work with engineers and scientists and free the latter of many routine tasks. Their work is technical in nature and they often assist the engineers and scientists in the areas of research, development and design work. They help, too, in various aspects of production planning, quality control, time and motion studies and problems pertaining to installation and maintenance.

The specific functions of these technicians depend upon the area of technology in which they work. *Aeronautical and aerospace technicians* assist engineers in many aspects of aircraft and spacecraft design and production engineering. *Agricultural technicians* help with the solution of problems concerning the scientific production and processing of food and other things that grow.

NONTRADITIONAL CAREERS FOR WOMEN

Air-conditioning, heating and refrigeration technicians work with engineers and scientists in one or more of the many areas of research, development and design of cooling, heating and refrigeration systems. *Automotive technicians* concentrate their activities on the improvement of today's cars and the perfection of the cars of tomorrow.

Chemical technicians specialize in chemical technology and are concerned with chemical products and equipment, and the development, production, sale and utilization of these products and equipment. *Civil engineering technicians* work with civil engineers and assist them with the miscellaneous tasks in the planning and construction of airports, bridges, dams, highways, railroads, viaducts and other structures. *Computer technicians* help computer engineers in the design and development of new and improved computers and varied electronic data-processing machines.

Ecology technicians assist scientists and engineers in combating the pollution crisis, improving our environment and protecting our natural resources. *Electronics technicians* belong to the ever-enlarging industry which encompasses electronic devices, ranging all the way from the very latest satellite communications systems to the tiny transistor radio, and they aid electronics engineers in many aspects of this area of technology.

Industrial technicians work with industrial engineers to develop improved production methods and thereby increase the productivity of industry. *Instrumentation technicians* are members of a very new and growing area of technology involving automatic controls and precision measuring devices, and they help in the development, design and research of these controls, devices and other highly complex instruments.

Mechanical technicians help mechanical engineers with the design and development of machinery and other equipment and parts; they include the *diesel technicians, machine designers* and *tool designers. Metallurgical technicians* concentrate their activities on the processing of metals and the conversion of these metals into finished products. *Meteorological technicians* work with meteorologists and assist them with research projects and in observing and describing atmospheric phenomena.

Nuclear engineering technicians assist nuclear engineers on research projects in the field of nuclear energy and also work with them on the design, development and production of nuclear devices and atomic power plants. *Radio and television broadcasting technicians* assist the engineers in the engineering departments of radio and television stations and help them set up, operate and maintain equipment in the studios and, when necessary, at outside locations. *Safety technicians* concentrate on the reduction of industrial hazards and, in the atomic energy field, are concerned with such matters as radiation safety, inspection and decontamination.

You can become a technician by completing a year or two of specialized, post–high school training, in contrast to the many years of college and university level training required of scientists and engineers. This post–high school training may be obtained in technical institutes, junior or community colleges or vocational schools. Many of these training programs are offered in evening sessions, enabling you to work during the daytime, after your high school graduation, and to receive your technical training in the evening.

You may obtain a list of the names and addresses of the approved technical institutes and schools by writing to the Engineers' Council for Professional Development, 345 East 47th St., New York, N.Y. 10017, and to the National Council of Technical Schools, 1835 K St. N.W., Washington, D.C. 20006.

You may be interested in any one of the many two-year technical curricula offered by the junior and community colleges. For information about these two-year programs leading to the associate degree in engineering technology, see this writer's book on paraprofessions mentioned earlier.

NONTRADITIONAL CAREERS FOR WOMEN

Do you enjoy tinkering with things? Do you possess mechanical aptitude and manual dexterity? Are you able to dismantle small appliances to determine how they work and then put them back in working condition again? Do you like to solve mathematical problems? If your answers to these questions are "Yes," then engineering technology may be the occupational field for you.

The majority of technicians work in manufacturing firms, communications, electrical equipment, aerospace and chemical industries and with the federal government. Employment opportunities for women as engineering and science technicians appear to be very good for the remainder of the 1970s. By 1980, it is anticipated, there will be a need for approximately 1,500,000 technicians, and women will be warmly welcomed to help meet this need. If you are trained to be a technician, you will become a member of one of the fastest-growing occupational groups and your occupational future should be indeed bright.

Female technicians belong to the American Society of Certified Engineering Technicians on an equal basis with male technicians. For further details about careers as technicians and information about certification in this field, write to the American Society of Certified Engineering Technicians, ASCET Information Center, P.O. Box 40230, Everman, Tex. 76140, and the Institute for the Certification of Engineering Technicians, 2029 K St. N.W., Washington, D.C. 20006.

The field of architecture is allied to the field of engineering. It involves several professional and paraprofessional careers included in the process of construction and design; among these are *architects, architectural technicians, landscape architects, urban planners* and *urban planning technicians.*

Architects plan and design structures of all types. The client who commissions them to design a building explains the purpose of the desired structure. They then proceed to plan and draw up the specifications of the building or other structure that will serve the client's purpose and be safe and attractive in appearance.

In 1971, there were about 35,000 licensed architects in the United States. The exact number of women architects at work throughout the nation is not available, but in 1971 about 300 women were members of the American Society of Architects. However, in that same year, female students represented 6.5 per cent of the total number of architectural students in this country. So the very low percentage of women in this field is on its way up—as it well should be, for this is a very attractive field for women.

Most architectural schools offer five-year programs leading to the degree of bachelor of architecture. High school graduates who seek admission to these schools must meet the entrance requirements of the college or university with which the school of architecture is associated. Some architectural schools offer a three- or four-year professional program, but require the successful completion of one or two years of prearchitectural college education for admission.

Every state and the District of Columbia require that architects be licensed to practice. Each individual state sets its own requirements for admission to the licensing examination. About 40 per cent of all architects are self-employed; others work for architectural firms, engineers, builders, real estate firms and government agencies.

Have you gazed at homes, office buildings, houses of worship, housing projects or other structures and thought, "I could have designed something more pleasant in appearance than that"? Are you able to visualize a structure in all its dimensions? Do you have creative talent? Can you draw well? Are you capable of handling technical problems? Do you have mathematical aptitude? If your replies are "Yes," you may want to become involved in truly building a better future by entering the architectural profession.

143

The employment outlook in this field is bright for the years ahead. Rapid growth in nonresidential as well as residential construction is anticipated. Shelter, a basic necessity of life, is a major concern of women. Women's ideas are needed in this field, and future employment opportunities look very favorable for female architects.

Further information about the career of the architect plus a list of architectural schools accredited by the National Architectural Accrediting Board may be obtained from the American Institute of Architects, 1785 Massachusetts Ave. N.W., Washington, D.C. 20036.

Perhaps you are fascinated by the field of architecture, but do not want to study so many years after your high school graduation. If so, you might want to become an *architectural technician* instead. To become an architectural technician, after completing your high school education, you need to study for only two years at a junior or community college in a training program leading to the associate degree in architectural technology.

Architectural technicians work with architects and perform a variety of services, depending on the size and nature of the architectural firm for which they work and the specialty of the architect with whom they work. By performing a miscellany of subprofessional tasks, they free the architect to concentrate on more complex activities.

The need for architectural technicians is great and training and employment opportunities for women as architectural technicians are very favorable. Would you like to know more about this career? Then read this writer's book on paraprofessions mentioned earlier.

Urban planning is a relatively new field. The career of the *urban planner* is a young one, and that of the *urban planning technician* is even younger.

The work of the urban planner is closely related to that of the architect. Urban planners are concerned about the growth and development of our cities. They develop plans and programs to revitalize the urban communities of our nation. Deteriorating business and residential areas, air pollution, shortage of parks and recreation facilities and traffic congestion are among the problems which they aim to remedy.

There were about 8,000 professional urban planners at work in the United States in 1971; of this number, about 10 per cent were women. In the main, they were employed by government agencies, metropolitan regional planning organizations, large land developers, private research organizations, consulting firms and colleges and universities.

Are you sensitive to the needs of your city and your community? Are you eager to work toward realistic goals to improve urban conditions and to stem the tide of deterioration? Do you have practical visual imagination? Would you be able to cope with the frustration often involved in planning urban projects and waiting for them to be completed? If so, you may have a bright future ahead of you as an urban planner.

To become an urban planner, you must complete your undergraduate college education with major study in a related field, such as economics, public administration, sociology, architecture, landscape architecture or engineering, and then continue on to graduate school to obtain a master's degree in urban planning.

There is a shortage of professionally trained urban planners, and employment prospects are very good for those who have the master's degree. Women should be concerned about improving the living conditions in our congested urban communities. If they obtain the required professional training, they should find in this field a very favorable employment future, with many stimulating tasks awaiting them.

Would you like further details about careers in urban planning and a list of schools offering professional training in this field? Then write to the American Institute of Planners, 917 15th St.

N.W., Washington, D.C. 20005, and to the American Society of Planning Officials, 1313 E. 60th St., Chicago, Ill. 60637.

If urban planning interests you, but you do not wish to go to college for your bachelor's and then your master's degree, give thought to a career as an *urban planning technician.* Only two years of study beyond high school is needed for entry into this career. To qualify for this career, you must successfully complete a two-year college program in urban planning technology and receive your associate degree.

Urban planning technicians work with urban planners and perform a variety of subprofessional functions, such as making neighborhood surveys, collecting pertinent information, analyzing this information and assisting as a member of a working team with urban planners, architects, government officials and others.

Urban planning technicians are as yet few in number, for theirs is such a fledgling career. However, the growth of new cities and towns, increasing numbers of urban renewal projects and a variety of urban development and beautification projects throughout the 1970s and into the 1980s will intensify the need for urban planners and with this an accompanying need for urban planning technicians. Employment prospects for women to fill these needs should be very good.

If the career of the urban planning technician sounds appealing to you and you would like further information about it, consult this writer's book on paraprofessions mentioned earlier.

Allied to the work of the urban planner and the architect is the work of the *landscape architect* and the *surveyor.*

Landscape architects plan and design the development of land areas for a miscellany of projects, such as airports, country clubs, highways, parks and other recreational facilities, parkways, schools and commercial, industrial and residential sites. They aim to design useful and attractive landscapes.

It was estimated that there were approximately 10,000 land-

146

scape architects at work in 1972; women comprised between 15 and 20 per cent of the total number of members and affiliates of the American Society of Landscape Architects. The majority of these landscape architects were self-employed or were employed by private landscape architectural firms; others worked for government agencies, engineering firms and colleges and universities.

The minimum requirement for entry into this profession is the bachelor's degree in landscape architecture. Young women who have artistic and designing talent and an interest in art and nature might well find this a very appealing profession. Here they will have the opportunity to use their ability to create pleasing and functional land areas. Many women tend to become specialists in garden and planting design.

Employment opportunities for women landscape architects appear to be excellent for the remainder of the 1970s and looking ahead into the 1980s. At present, there are not enough qualified women landscape architects to meet the demands for their services.

If you would like further information about this profession and a list of colleges and universities offering accredited curricula in landscape architecture, write to the American Society of Landscape Architects, 1750 Old Meadow Road, McLean, Va. 22101.

Surveyors work outdoors and their work is considered strenuous. As a result, women have not been welcome in this field; of some 50,000 surveyors who were at work in 1970, less than 5 per cent were women.

Surveyors determine the precise locations and measurements of points, elevations, lines, areas and contours of the earth's surface and the distance between certain points. They make these measurements for construction, mapmaking, land valuation, mining and varied other purposes. By gathering together information

147

on measurements and physical characteristics of construction sites, they play important roles in the construction of airfields, bridges, dams, highways and other structures.

If strenuous outdoor work does not faze you and you think you would like surveying, after your high school graduation you should enter a technical institute, vocational school or junior college one- or two-year training program in surveying. You should follow this with on-the-job training in survey techniques and in the use of survey instruments. Surveyors work for government agencies, surveying firms, construction companies and engineering and architectural firms.

Highway construction and urban development will stimulate the demand for surveyors for the remainder of the 1970s.

For details about a career in surveying and training opportunities in this field, write to the American Congress on Surveying and Mapping, 733 15th St. N.W., Washington, D.C. 20005.

The *technical writer* is a member of the family of engineering and scientific personnel. As a writer, she belongs too, and perhaps more properly, to the category of creative personnel and, therefore, is discussed in the chapter that follows.

Chapter 8

WRITING, CREATING AND COMMUNICATING

YOU have creative talents—and there is always someone discouraging you from using these talents, isn't there?

Don't let this bother you. Men too are very often discouraged from attempting to enter any of the creative fields. Of course, women are even more often discouraged than men.

Most people are afraid of failure. They don't use their native abilities and they discourage others, for they are afraid that others may succeed where they had feared to tread and this would intensify their feelings of failure. If you are convinced you have aptitude in any of the creative areas, DON'T LET ANYONE DISCOURAGE YOU!

Give yourself a chance! If you don't, no one else will.

Writing may be what *you* dream of doing. Those who may want to prevent your dream from coming true may tell you that down through the ages there were few women writers. Would you like to answer these people as they should be answered? Then ask them the following questions.

How many times have you read a poem or a story or a wise saying by "anonymous"? Many, many times—haven't you? Yes, "anonymous" is credited with a great many writings. Well, now, who do you think "anonymous" was? None other than Ann Onymous!

All right, perhaps the above is apocryphal. But there is no doubt that many "anonymous" authors were women. Until quite recently, women who wished to earn a living by their writings used masculine pseudonyms or used the initial in place of their first names, or, if they wrote for newspapers, sometimes their stories carried no by-lines at all. George Eliot, as you may know, was a woman by the name of Mary Ann Evans.

The first novel published in America was written by a woman, Sarah Wentworth Apthorp Morton. The book was published in Boston in 1789 and was called *The Power of Sympathy or the Triumph of Nature Founded in Truth*. However, since the author was a woman, it was published under the pseudonym of "Philenia" rather than her actual name.

Well, today you need not deny your femininity. You can write and be proud to declare yourself a woman!

Now, if you dream of being a *writer*, the first thing to do is stop dreaming and write! Remember that not only was the first American novelist a woman, but one of the foremost writers of this century was a woman—Pearl Buck!

What would *you* like to write? Would you like to be an *author* of nonfiction books, a *novelist*, a *playwright*, a *short story writer?* There are many different types of writers. The term "author" actually is applied to persons who write all types of literary works, such as articles, books, essays, plays and poems.

Among the many varieties of authors are the *free-lance article writers*, who submit their articles for publication in magazines and other periodicals; the *novelists*, who write books of fiction; the *playwrights* (also known as *dramatists*), who write original plays; the *poets*, who compose narrative, dramatic or lyric poetry; the *songwriters* (also known as *lyricists*), who write words to be spoken or sung to the accompaniment of music; and the *short story writers*, who write fictional tales for miscellaneous periodicals and books. If you have the ability to write humorous or sentimental verse, you might want to become a *greeting card writer* in your spare time.

In many creative fields, such as the aforementioned, the talented persons are not seeking positions, but instead are aiming to sell the products of their creativity. Therefore, entry into these fields is not obtained by the usual job-seeking methods, but by knowing how to market your talents. If you want to become an author, you must accept the reality of rejection slips. This means that you will probably write thousands and thousands of words before a publisher buys what you have written. But the more you write, if you have talent, the more you will perfect your writing and the more skilled you will become at this art.

You may have read of a "first novel" which became an overnight success and brought fast fame and fortune to the author. Don't believe it! This has rarely, if ever, happened. This "first novel" was probably the fourth or fifth or possibly even the fifteenth written by that author; the earlier novels, plus perhaps a number of short stories and articles, written by that same author were probably rejected by many publishers.

Thomas Wolfe's *Look Homeward Angel* was rejected by a dozen publishers before it was accepted and became a success. Every successful author has lived through the trauma of rejection slips, and many could plaster their living room walls with the rejection slips they received before they met with success. Even after an author succeeds in having a manuscript accepted by a publisher, she lives in prayerful hopes that the published product will receive good reviews and be, if not a "best seller," at least a good seller.

George Bernard Shaw wrote four novels, all of which failed. When he turned to the theater and playwriting, he found the branch of writing suited to his talents and there he met success. You too must discover which branch of writing is most suited to your individual creative talents.

So, if you have writing ability, if, as your own boss, you can discipline yourself to the task of sticking to your typewriter when friends or relatives are coaxing you to go elsewhere with them and if you truly enjoy writing, then go ahead and write and write and write. Practice is essential. When you have written something you think is publishable, then you must learn how to prepare the manuscript and how to market it.

For help on how and where to sell what you have written, read the *Writer's Digest,* a monthly magazine, and *Writer's Market,* an annual publication, both published by Writer's Digest, 22 East 12th St., Cincinnati, Ohio 45210. Additionally, read *Literary Market Place (LMP);* you should be able to find a copy of this book in your local public library, or else write to the publisher, R. R. Bowker Co., 1180 Avenue of the Americas, New York, N.Y. 10036.

You may hear or read about publishing houses that will publish your book if you pay them a specified price. Such publishing houses are called "vanity presses." Unless you are rich and have money to squander to pamper your vanity, stay away from the vanity presses. If you have written a book which is worthy of publication, you will not need to pay anyone to publish it; on the contrary, a publisher will pay you.

There is no specific preparation for entry into the writing profession. Writing is a talent that is polished by practice, and the polishing is essentially self-taught. However, it is advisable that you get a good four-year liberal arts college education and learn all you can about the world around you, about people, places and things. Although it is not necessary, you may find it desirable to take courses in creative writing and the marketing of manuscripts. If you would like to write nonfiction articles and books, you should become an expert in a specific field, and for this a master's or doctor's degree in that field is desirable.

Every author has her tale of how she earned her first check from the fruits of her writing. My first check was $1 for a poem

I submitted to a women's magazine when I was a college freshman. No dollar earned since then has ever brought so much gratification. Later poems brought $5 or $10 or just a subscription to the magazine which published the poem. Several years later, when I became a guidance counselor, I wrote short stories and articles for teen-agers. These were followed by my first book in the field of guidance—and what a thrill that was! Then came the second book, and then came many more.

If poetry is your primary writing interest, then read and be inspired by the poetry of Edna St. Vincent Millay, the first woman to receive the Pulitzer Prize for poetry. In 1950, Gwendolyn Brooks became the first black woman to be awarded the Pulitzer Prize for poetry. This brilliant poet has received many other awards for her writings, including the Guggenheim Fellowship for creative writing, and in 1968 she was named the Poet Laureate of Illinois. Her autobiography, *Report from Part One* (Broadside Press, Detroit, 1972), is a most interesting, inspiring volume; all who aspire to become poets should read it.

It takes years of practice to develop proficiency in the art of writing. If you are determined to become an author and are convinced you have writing talent, don't get discouraged and don't let rejection slips depress you. Writing is a very difficult field in which to gain success. Many, many people want to become authors, but only a limited number succeed. So, while you are trying to sell your stories or articles or that all-American best-selling novel which everyone dreams of writing, it is highly advisable that you also have some marketable skill at which you can earn an income until your writings start to produce cashable checks rather than rejection slips.

It is estimated that there are about twice as many male authors as female. Talent knows no gender, so that has nothing to do with writing aptitude, but rather with the fact that women have not attempted to enter this field in the same numbers as men have. If you would like to obtain information from the professional association of authors, write to the Authors League of America, Inc. (which includes the Authors Guild and the Dramatists Guild), 234 West 44th St., New York, N.Y. 10036.

Many young women who have creative ability decide to enter the editing, rather than the writing, branch of publishing and work on a salaried basis as employees of publishing houses. *Book editors* interview authors, decide on topics for books, negotiate with authors on matters pertaining to publication of their books, suggest certain changes in book manuscripts and in many other ways work together with the authors and members of the publishing house to produce a book in published form.

There are no exact figures available on the number of book editors, but it is known that women are well represented in this field and there should be expanding opportunities for them in the years ahead. Women editors, as a matter of fact, predominate in the publishing of children's books. You may wish to contact the Women's National Book Association, c/o National Book Committee, 2 Park Ave., New York, N.Y. 10016.

Probably the largest group of salaried writers are the *journalists*. Actually, the title "journalist" is applied to any *editor* or *writer* performing editing or writing functions for newspapers or periodicals. They are often classified by the subject matter they edit or write; thus, the *financial editor* directs a newspaper or magazine department dealing with financial and business news. Another classification is based on the function they perform, such as the *newspaper reporter*.

Newspaper reporters collect and analyze information about current events by means of interviews, investigations or observation and use this information to write stories for publication in newspapers. *Feature reporters* write stories or other newspaper pieces which emphasize their writing style and personal viewpoint.

A special type of newspaper reporter who reports stories and news items by telephone, telegraph or other means from locations distant from the publisher's home base is the *newspaper corre-*

spondent; those who are stationed overseas are called *foreign correspondents.*

There are also the *columnists.* Columnists write feature columns which appear periodically in newspapers or magazines; they may comment on events, persons or places of athletic, economic, political or social interest. They are often known by the type of columns they write, such as *fashion columnist, political columnist* and *sports columnist.*

There were about 40,000 newspaper reporters at work for daily newspapers, weekly newspapers, press services and newspaper syndicates in the United States in 1971; more than one-third of them were women. All of these women owe a great debt to the amazing Nellie Bly.

Elizabeth Cochrane was only eighteen years of age when she won a battle of wits and words and convinced the editor of the *Pittsburgh Dispatch,* George Madden, to hire her as a reporter. He was determined, however, that her stories appear under a masculine name rather than her own. After another skirmish, they finally compromised by agreeing that she use the name Nellie Bly, from the popular song written by Stephen Foster. When did all this take place? Long before today's Women's Lib movement—back in 1885, almost one hundred years ago!

Nellie Bly later went to New York and convinced Joseph Pulitzer to appoint her to the reportorial staff of the *World,* the great newspaper of that day. She became the first female foreign correspondent and accomplished many astounding feats to get her feature stories. If you would like to become a newspaper reporter, go to your local public library and read about the amazing achievements of this unusual woman; they may inspire you to go and do likewise.

To enter the field of journalism, it is desirable that you have a bachelor's degree, preferably with a major in journalism. Favorable employment opportunities as newspaper reporters should be available throughout the remaining 1970s to well-qualified beginners who possess exceptional writing ability; those who are capable of handling news about highly specialized and technical topics should also find a favorable employment future.

For additional information about newspaper careers, write to the American Newspaper Publishers Association, 750 Third Ave., New York, N.Y. 10017, and the Newspaper Guild, 1126 16th St. N.W., Washington, D.C. 20036.

Perhaps you possess aptitude and interest in science and technology, and yet you do not want to enter any of the scientific and technological careers discussed in Chapters 6 and 7. But you also have writing ability and like to write. Then you may want to combine and put to use your scientific, technological and writing abilities. You can do this by becoming a *technical writer* or a *science writer.*

Technical writers write service manuals and related technical publications in concise and lucid language; they also organize, write and edit articles, stories and other materials about science and technology so that these materials are understandable to those who need to use this information. *Science writers* are technical writers who specialize in any one of the fields of science; among the science writers are the *medical writers,* who limit their technical writing and editing to topics of a health and medical nature.

In 1970, there were about 20,000 technical writers at work in the United States, and it was estimated that about one-third were women. Technical writers are employed by firms in the electronics and aerospace industries, research and development firms, government agencies and newspapers and other publications; a small number are self-employed as free-lance technical writers.

The minimum entrance requirement in this field is the bachelor's degree, preferably with a major in science or engineering. A combination of college courses in journalism, writing and scientific and technical subjects is desirable.

It is expected that well-qualified technical writers will find good employment opportunities available to them throughout the 1970s. Increasing numbers of women are entering this field. If you would like to bridge the communications gap between scientists, engineers and other people and if you are a competent writer, well trained in scientific and technical matters, there should be good employment prospects for you in the field of technical writing.

For further details about a career as a technical writer, write to the Society for Technical Communication, 1010 Vermont Ave. N.W., Suite 421, Washington, D.C. 20005.

There is another important group of professionals who are very much involved with books, magazines and other written and audiovisual materials. These are the *librarians*. Over 85 per cent of the estimated 125,000 professional librarians at work in libraries throughout the United States in 1971 were women. More of the administrative posts in large library systems were held by men than by women; however, the number of women being appointed to executive positions is increasing.

Since librarianship is thus traditionally very much a women's profession, we will not go into further detail about it here. Those who would like additional information about librarianship careers should write to the American Library Association, 50 E. Huron St., Chicago, Ill. 60611.

Perhaps you would like to become an *artist*. The art field encompasses women and men of diverse talents who earn their living in many different ways. You may dream of becoming *the painter* of *the painting* which will draw rave reviews from all the noted art critics.

The famous painters are, in the main, men. However, many women have artistic talent and there is no reason why they too cannot become accomplished painters. If you believe you have this talent and your art teachers agree with you, then go ahead and express your thoughts, ideas and experiences with paint, brush and other implements. You will need to paint and paint

157

and paint—and then paint some more; then select the best works you have created and gather them together into a portfolio.

This portfolio represents you and your talents, so put together the best possible portfolio including your best artistic productions. It is not easy for young painters to find art galleries or other places in which to exhibit their paintings. Gallery owners and other art exhibitors must be impressed with your portfolio before they will agree to show your work; they must be convinced that your paintings will receive the plaudits of art buyers and art collectors and could be sold at worth-while prices. Some gallery owners prefer to show the works of painters who specialize, such as *portrait painters* and *watercolor painters.*

You may have to pound the pavements, going from one art gallery to another and another and another, until you find a gallery owner who consents to exhibit the fruits of your talents. You then make an agreement with him to pay him a specified commission on the prices of any of your paintings that he may sell.

Now note this very important point: before you sign any agreement, get yourself a competent lawyer and have him read the agreement; DON'T sign anything without your lawyer's permission. This holds true not only for artists but also for writers, performers and all others who are self-employed and earn (or hope to earn) a living by selling the products of their personal creativity.

Since gallery owners are generally not too receptive to beginners, you would be wise to band together with other artists in your town or city and convince your local restaurateurs, theater managers, department store owners, the clergy and your local elected officials to permit you to exhibit your paintings in their restaurants, theater lobbies, department stores, church and synagogue bazaars and sidewalk displays. Be sure to do a good job publicizing these exhibits well in advance, notifying art dealers, gallery owners, museum curators and, of course, the local citizenry.

Back in 1889, five young women artists formed the Women's

Art Club of the City of New York. This club aimed to contend with the problems arising due to discrimination against women artists. As it grew in size and became nationwide in scope, it changed its name to the National Association of Women Artists, which now has a membership of over 700 professional artists. For further information, write to the National Association of Women Artists, Inc., 156 Fifth Ave., New York, N.Y. 10010.

It often takes many years of painting before painters receive recognition for their work and are capable of living solely on the income derived from their paintings. They generally, therefore, must find other employment until such time when their paintings can be sold at profitable prices. Some, who have completed the necessary education courses at college, may become *art teachers* and earn an income as teachers while painting on a free-lance basis; others may become *commercial artists.*

Commercial artists create illustrations and sketches for the purpose of making products, services and ideas more attractive to consumers. They are often known as *illustrators* because they draw and paint illustrations for advertisements, books, magazines, billboards, catalogues and posters.

There are many different types of commercial artists. *Advertising artists* plan and create miscellaneous promotional and publicity materials for the advertising agencies or other organizations by which they are employed. *Letterers* produce the appropriate lettering needed for varied items depending upon the nature of their employers. There are commercial artists who also work as *designers* and do many different types of designing for commercial purposes.

Book designers select the proper type and binding for the books published by their employers; they also design the jackets and covers for these books. *Magazine designers* create covers to make a magazine look as attractive as possible; they also aim to make the format, inside pages and back page eye-appealing, thereby to increase the number of sales of the magazine.

Package designers have a knowledge of merchandising which

they combine with their artistic talent to design packages so attractively that housewives and other purchasers will quickly remove these packages from the shelves of supermarkets and other stores. *Record jacket designers* plan and create the backs and fronts of the jackets of records.

Under the broad category of commercial artists are also the *greeting card artists;* they create the funny and serious drawings which appear on all sorts of greeting cards. There are too the *sign painters,* who create display cards, signs and posters, and the *display artists* and *window trimmers,* who plan and create displays designed to catch the eye of potential shoppers and to lure them into the store.

A unique type of commercial artist is the *cartoonist,* who draws cartoons for advertising, education, entertainment, news reporting, political, sports and television purposes. There are some cartoonists who work as *comic strip artists;* a story continuity accompanies the drawings in their daily newspaper strips.

There were about 60,000 miscellaneous commercial artists at work in 1970, and approximately 40 per cent of them were women. Commercial artists find employment opportunities in every large city and many smaller ones, but the greatest concentration of them is found in New York and Chicago in advertising agencies, commercial art studios, publishing houses, advertising departments of large companies, department stores, newspapers and television and motion-picture studios.

The basic requirement for entering the commercial art field is, of course, the possession of art aptitude. Also important are creative imagination, originality, good taste, a good color sense, some mechanical aptitude and finger dexterity. Commercial artists should also have a keen understanding of human needs and values.

Preparation for a career in commercial art starts with your high school art courses. This should be followed by study in an approved art school or institute specializing in commercial and applied art. Training in art schools, art departments of junior and community colleges or schools of fine arts may often be completed in two or three years; students may attend evening sessions while holding a full-time beginner's position in the field of art.

There are also many colleges and universities offering major curricula in art; the B.A. (bachelor of arts) or B.F.A. (bachelor of fine arts) is awarded upon successful completion of the four-year program, and either of these degrees is necessary if you would someday like to teach art.

The employment outlook is favorable for talented, well-trained commercial artists. Many salaried commercial artists also accept free-lance assignments in their spare time. Qualified women with family obligations could work at home on free-lance assignments and work as many hours as their home responsibilities permit. A portfolio of your best illustrations will be a great help in enabling you to obtain free-lance assignments.

For additional information about a career as a commercial artist and a list of approved art schools, write to the Society of Illustrators, 128 East 63rd St., New York, N.Y. 10021. You might also like to write to the Magazine Cartoonists Guild, 220 West 78th St., New York, N.Y. 10024, and the National Association of Greeting Card Publishers, 30 Rockefeller Plaza, New York, N.Y. 10020.

The small field of industrial design offers employment opportunities to those who have art aptitude plus technical knowledge of materials, machines and methods of production. *Industrial designers* aim to improve the appearance and functional design of their employers' products so these products may outsell similar products on the market. They design a wide variety of products including furniture, household appliances, lamps, motor vehicles, radio and television cabinets and stereo sets.

Industrial designers are also known as *product designers*. There were about 10,000 of them at work in 1970, and only a tiny percentage of them were women. The recommended preparation for entry into this field is the completion of a four-year college program in industrial design leading to a bachelor's degree. Women have had very limited opportunities in this field, but there will be increasing opportunities for exceptionally talented women in the years ahead, particularly in the areas of automotive interiors, furniture, packaging and showroom design.

Additional information about this field is available from the Industrial Designers Society of America, 60 West 55th St., New York, N.Y. 10019.

Another field of designing which offers job opportunities for those with artistic talent is that of interior design, which generally includes interior decoration.

Interior designers and *interior decorators* plan and design attractive, artistic interiors for homes, residential and commercial buildings, hotels, motels, institutions, ships, aircraft and miscellaneous other structures and establishments. They select and purchase decorative and functional materials and accessories, such as furniture, draperies, floor coverings, lighting fixtures and pictures. Sometimes one person works solely as an interior designer and concentrates on planning the functional arrangement of the interior space. Often, however, both the design and decoration are done by one individual titled *interior designer and decorator.*

Although men have begun to predominate in the field of interior design, traditionally interior decoration has been a women's field. In 1970, there were about 15,000 people at work on a fulltime basis in interior design and decoration; women represented about 50 per cent of them. Therefore, we will not go into further detail about this here. However, it should be noted that it is anticipated that artistically talented female high school graduates who are willing to spend three to four years in a professional school or college receiving specialized interior design and decoration training will have a bright employment future; increasing part-time employment opportunities will also be available to them, permitting them to combine career and family if they so desire.

Those who wish additional information about this field may obtain it from the National Society of Interior Designers, 315 East 62nd St., New York, N.Y. 10021.

Many women use their art aptitude and interest in the fashion field to become *fashion designers*. This is a highly competitive, traditionally women's field. If you would like details about a career in fashion designing, write to the Fashion Group, 9 Rockefeller Plaza, New York, N.Y. 10020.

Floral designers fashion attractive flower arrangements appropriate for whatever purpose the customer desires these bouquets, corsages or other arrangements. Women who have artistic ability can receive on-the-job training to do this work in retail florist shops. It is expected that employment of floral designers will increase very rapidly for the remainder of the 1970s. Detailed information about the career of the floral designer is available from the Society of American Florists and Ornamental Horticulturists, 901 N. Washington St., Alexandria, Va. 22314.

Beauticians (also known as *cosmetologists*) and *hairdressers* belong to the category of occupations called "service occupations." However, they may be included with creative occupations because their work entails a sense of artistry and creativity. They need the aptitude and dexterity to improve the appearance of each of their customers.

There were about half a million beauticians and hairdressers at work in 1971. Approximately 90 per cent of them were women. Cosmetology is most decidedly a traditional field for women. It is also an expanding field, and the employment future looks bright for those trained in cosmetology; additionally, there should be good opportunities for part-time work. If you would like additional information, write to the National Hairdressers and Cosmetologists Association, 175 Fifth Ave., New York, N.Y. 10010.

Women who have artistic ability plus manual dexterity, imagination, originality and the ability to put people at ease may want to consider a career in photography. *Photographers* need the aforementioned attributes plus technical skill in the use of cameras to photograph persons, places, animals, scenes and things.

The specific work performed by photographers depends upon their area of specialization. *Aerial photographers* take photographs from airplanes while in flight. *Commercial photographers* make photographs for advertising and sales purposes. *Industrial photographers* generally work for one particular company and take pictures for this company's publications and for other industrial purposes. *Motion picture photographers* concentrate their work activities on pictures taken with motion-picture cameras. *Portrait photographers* take natural-looking, attractive portraits of individuals. *Press photographers* (also known as *photojournalists*) take pictures of news events and of prominent persons in the news.

There are no specific requirements for becoming a professional photographer. Entry into this field may be through a variety of ways, such as two or three years of on-the-job training after high school, one or two years of specialized training in an approved technical institute, a two-year photography program in a junior or community college or a four-year college program with a photography major.

Photography is a popular hobby enjoyed by millions of amateur photographers, female as well as male. As an occupation, however, photography is a male-dominated field. The exact number of women professional photographers is unknown, but the number is small. In 1970, there were about 65,000 professional photographers at work throughout the United States, of whom only a tiny percentage were female. Women, however, have been among the outstanding photographers. Probably the most outstanding was Margaret Bourke-White.

Margaret Bourke-White used the camera to work her way

through college and became so enamored with photography that after her graduation from Cornell University, she became a professional photographer and made her mark in the field of photojournalism. During World War II and the Korean War, she risked her life many times to photograph battlefield and other historic actions which she thought should be recorded. She went where many others feared to go and was often commended for her heroic behavior. Her cameras became inactive when she died of Parkinsonism in August, 1971.

Not every photographer can become a Margaret Bourke-White, but talented, well-trained women should find many challenging opportunities available to them in this field in the years ahead. Those who also have good business ability could become self-employed as portrait photographers, particularly in taking pictures of babies and children in their community, on a part-time or full-time basis. If you would like further details about a career in photography and a list of approved schools of photography, write to Professional Photographers of America, Inc., 1090 Executive Way, Des Plaines, Ill. 60018.

The performing fields offer additional opportunities to women for careers in creating and communicating. *Performers* need abundant natural talent and tremendous persistence to succeed. Many young people aspire to careers in the performing arts, but success comes to a limited number only. Competition is exceptionally keen in these fields, for the number of people seeking to enter these fields usually far exceed the number of positions available.

Essentially, the performing arts include acting, dancing, music and singing. In a broader sense, however, they also encompass the motion pictures, radio and television and sports fields.

Actresses work mainly in legitimate theaters, motion pictures, radio and television. They make a character come to life. They need a great deal of versatility, skill, the ability to project and physical stamina for auditions and rehearsals.

165

NONTRADITIONAL CAREERS FOR WOMEN

Professional dancers perform alone, with a partner or as a member of a group in the theater, musical shows, operas, concerts and on television. Many years of practice and performance are needed before dancers become skilled in their art.

Musicians may play one or more musical instruments as soloists or as members of bands, orchestras or other musical groups; they may be known by the instrument they play most often, such as the *drummers, pianists* and *violinists. Singers* are also called *vocalists,* and they may give solo performances or sing with a band, chorus, orchestra or other vocal group.

For further details about careers in the performing arts, you may wish to write to any one or more of the following: Actors Equity Association, 165 West 46th St., New York, N.Y. 10036; American Federation of Musicians, 641 Lexington Ave., New York, N.Y. 10022; American Guild of Musical Artists, 1841 Broadway, New York, N.Y. 10023.

The motion-picture industry and the broadcasting industry employ a variety of performers and other creative personnel, in addition to those already mentioned. These so-called glamour industries attract large numbers of young people, but only a few are fortunate enough to find full-time employment.

Motion-picture narrators (known too as *motion-picture commentators*) make comments which explain and accompany the action parts of the film. *Motion-picture projectionists* set up and operate the motion-picture projection and sound-reproducing equipment in order to project coordinated picture and sound effects on the screen; they are also known as *cinematographers. Scenario writers* write stories, screen adaptations or scenarios for motion pictures; they may revise the script during production as suggested by the *motion-picture directors* or *motion-picture producers.*

There are expanding employment opportunities for women in the growing field of educational films.

W.O.M.P.I. (Women of the Motion Picture Industry) is the ser-

166

vice organization of women in this industry; for further information, write to Hilda Frishman, International President, Women of the Motion Picture Industry, International, c/o United Artists Corporation, 729 Seventh Ave., New York, N.Y. 10019.

There is a variety of radio and television broadcasting personnel. Women represented about 25 per cent of the estimated 120,000 full-time broadcasting staff members in 1971. They included a miscellany of broadcast personnel.

Announcers introduce programs, guests and musical selections; they often deliver the commercial messages. *Continuity writers* prepare material that is read on the air to introduce and connect parts of musical, news and sports programs. *Directors* plan and supervise individual programs or series of programs; they give directions to members of the cast and technical crew during the rehearsals and the broadcasting of radio and television programs. *Film editors* edit and prepare films for presentation on television. *Makeup artists* apply appropriate makeup to those who are scheduled to appear on television broadcasts.

Newscasters broadcast the daily news programs. *Newswriters* select and write the news copy which will be read on the air by the newscasters. *News correspondents* and *news commentators* (also called *news analysts*) analyze, interpret and broadcast news received from a variety of sources. Competition for positions in the broadcasting industry is extremely keen. It takes superior talent for a woman to succeed in this industry. When this woman is also black and she succeeds as a television news correspondent, she must be quite unusual. Joan Murray, a dynamic, articulate young lady, is considered the first accredited black female television news correspondent in the United States.

Ms. Murray has appeared on many news, public affairs, documentary and other programs. She was selected as one of the "Foremost Women in Communications" (1969-70). Recently, she also branched out into black entrepreneurship to become co-founder and Executive Vice-President of ZEBRA Associates, the

Nation's largest black-owned and -managed advertising agency.

"I was born in Ithaca, New York, an upstate college town where Cornell University is located," says Ms. Murray. "It's a pleasant, outdoorsy kind of place, and coupled with its small-town atmosphere and blessed with unusual parents . . . I had a terrific childhood. After high school, my twin sister, June, decided to work and continue her education in New York City. We're identical twins and, naturally, I was lonely without her. And so, after finishing a year at Ithaca College, I followed her to the Big City. Fortunately, I had learned typing and shorthand when only fourteen years of age . . . skills, by the way, which have benefited me all my career life. As a matter of fact, when I was just fifteen, I had my first part-time job as a secretary to a law professor at Cornell."

"Initially, my secretarial skills enabled me to find employment in a theatrical agency not long after I arrived in New York," Ms. Murray continues. "From there, I decided to move into something more to my liking, especially since I still had plans of becoming a court reporter. Then, one day, I noticed an ad in the newspapers, and applied for a secretarial position at the Columbia Broadcasting System (CBS). Because of my special expertise in shorthand and typing, I was placed in the CBS Network TV Press and Publicity Department."

"From this inside view and having the privilege of working with fantastic writers," she says, "my aspirations shifted from court reporting to electronic journalism. Immediately, I knew that working in CBS Press was the right atmosphere for me. Most of the key people in the field are flexible writers and their livelihood depends upon conception of thought, and writing these ideas via the typewriter. So often, even today, I can 'think better on my typewriter'!"

"I cannot stress too strongly," Ms. Murray emphasizes, "how valuable basic skills and common sense can be to a young person who wants a career in television or, for that matter, any type of business. Basic skills, like shorthand and typing, will always help you, at least, get your foot into the door. And don't forget the hard work. When I began at CBS, I didn't mind working all sorts of hours, coming in early, staying late or taking on any extra duties in TV Press. You tend to learn quicker this way, too, and with this comes a sense of accomplishment and self-confidence . . . much needed assets in the field of television."

Ms. Murray adds: "I believe that once you've learned as much as you can and your abilities outgrow the job, it's time to move on to more and better challenges. Accordingly, I worked on many different assignments and programs and in the process learned a lot about film editing, script writing and producing (for instance, CBS Corporate Information, Allen Funt's 'Candid Camera' show, NBC-TV and WCBS-TV news). This was tough, because at the time, I was also busy taking evening courses toward a degree in journalism. Furthering one's education and knowing what's going on in the world (I used to read as many as fifteen national and international newspapers a day), as well as being able to write well and speak properly, are essential in television. And don't forget a pleasant, self-confident and well-groomed appearance . . . both on and off the camera. Sloppiness won't do.

"Men don't have to be as concerned about how they look on camera as women do. You want to look attractive, not only for yourself but for the viewing audience as well. If you look careless, your appearance may distract from an all-important news story. Also, there's a lot of talk today about the problems a woman has in competing in a man's world. I personally feel that a businesswoman finds it much easier if she remains really feminine (but not coy) than if she tries to be 'one of the boys.' If a young woman is ladylike, well mannered, assertive but not overly aggressive and proves herself competent on the job, she will be accepted and not resented by men in the industry. If you respect yourself, you'll gain respect."

Joan Murray concludes, "I've had the opportunity, in spite of a great deal of discrimination and prejudice towards women and blacks, to function in an industry I love and to meet and interview interesting people from all walks of life . . . as a matter of fact, people who range from Dr. Martin Luther King, Jr., to Flip Wilson, from Presidents Eisenhower to Kennedy, from Ingrid Bergman to Lady Bird Johnson. I've covered stories that include women's prisons, assassinations and even learned to pilot a small plane for a documentary series on aircraft."

She emphasizes, "It's a fantastically satisfying and rewarding career, if you're willing to work at it and you love the business of television!"

There are yet other people who play important roles in the broadcasting industry. *Program assistants* help by carrying out the orders of the *directors* and the *associate directors*. *Program directors* are responsible for the over-all program schedules of large radio or television stations. *Radio engineers* (also known as *station engineers*) operate and maintain station audio and video transmission equipment in accord with Federal regulations. *Radio and television producers* plan, coordinate and are responsible for the over-all problems of radio and television program production.

Scenic designers plan and design the backgrounds and settings for television programs. *Script writers* originate the theme and dialogue for sketches, plays and similar types of programs. *Sound effects technicians* operate special equipment to simulate sounds needed for specific radio and television programs.

Increasing opportunities are opening up for women in all capacities in the broadcasting industry. Their best opportunities have long been as performers and program directors on women's news shows, interview shows and talk shows.

Further information about careers in the field of radio and television is available from the National Association of Broadcasters, 1771 N St. N.W., Washington, D.C. 20036. In 1951, women working as broadcasters, executives, creative personnel and in miscellaneous other aspects of this industry established their own organization, American Women in Radio and Television, as a means of communicating with each other and exchanging industry ideas; for details about A.W.R.T. and its materials on careers for women in broadcasting, write to American Women in Radio and Television, Inc., 1321 Connecticut Ave. N.W., Washington, D.C. 20036.

The performing occupations appeal to a great many young people. There are those who undergo privation and years of painstaking practice in an attempt to reach perfection in the performing arts, and nonetheless do not achieve their goals because of the extremely keen competition. Few have the abundant talent and the abundant determination which are imperative to gain and keep employment as professional performers.

Do you have this talent and determination? If so, get as much experience as possible in these arts by participating in your school's and/or community's dramatic, musical and similar events. Although there are no specific educational requirements for entry into many of the performing occupations, a college education with major study in broadcasting, dramatic arts, journalism or motion pictures is desirable.

Above all, be sure to develop a marketable skill at which you can earn a living while you are trying to enter the highly competitive performing arts fields and, at the same time, prepare for a second occupation at which you could become gainfully employed if you are unable to enter the performing occupation of your choice.

The sports fields are generally categorized as belonging to the physical education and recreation occupations. However, *professional athletes* are certainly performers. There are now female *professional baseball players* and *professional football players*, but so far they are playing only on all-girl teams. All-girl football

171

teams are forming throughout the nation; at present, these teams include the New York Fillies, the Pittsburgh Powderkegs, the Detroit Cowgirls and the Cleveland Daredevils.

There are no restrictions in the National Basketball Association constitution and by-laws that would prevent a qualified young woman from playing in the N.B.A.; for further information about this matter, write to the National Basketball Association, 2 Pennsylvania Plaza, Suite 2360, New York, N.Y. 10001.

The best opportunities for women athletes are in those sports where they can engage in individual competition, such as *professional golf* and *professional tennis,* rather than as team members.

Some women might like to become *coaches* or *umpires* rather than active participants in a specific sport. In January, 1972, the highest court of the State of New York ruled that a woman could not be denied the right to be a *professional baseball umpire* because of her sex.

Proper muscular coordination, agility, above-average strength and excellent health are essential for success as a professional athlete, as are rigorous training and practice.

Athletes have only a short span of years during which they can actively, professionally engage in their sport, and this holds true for women as well as for men. Opportunities are opening for women in baseball, basketball, bowling, football, golf, swimming and tennis. The opportunities are limited and probably will remain limited for quite some time. But if you have athletic ability and wish to become a professional athlete, then go to it, push the doors open further and good luck to you!

The all-encompassing, euphemistic term for the performing occupations is "show business." It is said that there's no business like show business. Well, there is a great big world of business, very much unlike show business, and it offers many hundreds of thousands of employment opportunities to women. Let's look in on that world.

Chapter 9

THE BUSINESS WORLD

MILLIONS of women are in the business world. The great majority of them are *office workers*—secretaries and stenographers, bookkeepers, typists, telephone operators, receptionists and miscellaneous clerical workers. These workers are classified under the broad category of "clerical and related occupations."

Over 13,000,000 persons were engaged in some type of clerical or related activity in 1972. It may be said that these *clerical workers* oil the wheels of modern business. They do this by their record keeping, office management and performance of an endless variety of office tasks.

More than two-thirds of all those who hold these "clerical and related positions" are women. In some occupations, the percentage of women is even higher. Thus, of the almost 3,000,000 *stenographers* and *secretaries* at work in 1972, over 95 per cent were women; of about 1,500,000 *bookkeeping workers,* 90 per cent were women; of some 850,000 *cashiers,* about 90 per cent were women; of about 700,000 *typists,* more than 95 per cent were women; almost all of the 420,000 *telephone operators* were women; of about 375,000 *office machine operators,* approximately 75 per cent were women; of some 300,000 *reception: ,* over 95 per cent were women.

On the whole, there is a favorable employment outlook for most

173

"clerical and related occupations," with the most rapid employment growth and brightest future for the secretaries and stenographers and the most moderate growth for the bookkeeping workers. Since these are all traditionally "women's jobs," we will not go into further detail about them here.

For information about private business schools where training for entry into these "clerical and related occupations" may be obtained, write to the United Business Schools Association, 1730 M St. N.W., Washington, D.C. 20036. If you would like to become a certified professional secretary, write for information to the Institute for Certifying Secretaries, 616 East 63rd St., Kansas City, Mo. 64110.

The door that leads into the business world is the door of the personnel department. When a young woman applies to the personnel department of the firm for which she would like to work, she is all too often directed toward one of the traditional "women's jobs." Frequently, she must start as a typist or secretary and prove herself in these positions before she has any opportunity to enter upon the specific occupation for which she was trained.

The personnel departments of business organizations have long been the focal point of this problem. Most of these departments have been male-dominated, and the men who did the hiring directed female job applicants to so-called female jobs. More women are needed in the personnel administration profession to prevent a continuation of this practice, for despite the laws against sexist discrimination many firms are using all sorts of ruses to circumvent the laws.

There were approximately 160,000 *personnel workers* employed in the United States in 1970, and only about 25 per cent of them were women.

There are many different personnel workers who together constitute the personnel department. This department aims to recruit and hire capable employees and place them in positions most suited to their training and abilities; it also performs many other functions all designed to keep the organization of which it is a part running smoothly and effectively.

At the start of 1973, there were approximately 83,000,000 persons at work in the United States. The great majority of them, especially those who were employed by large business enterprises, industrial organizations and government agencies, had to pass through their employer's personnel department. Essentially, this department serves as a liaison between the employees and the employer.

Aside from the *personnel assistants* and *personnel clerks* who are clerical workers and generally female, there are the *personnel recruiters,* who visit schools and colleges to recruit competent job candidates for their employers; the *personnel interviewers,* who interview job applicants; the *psychometricians (psychological testers),* who administer psychological and vocational tests to applicants; the *training assistants* and *training specialists,* who train new employees; the *employee counselors,* who aid employees with their individual problems; the *employee relations specialists,* who are concerned with the morale of the employees; and the *labor relations specialists,* who attempt to maintain peace between labor and management.

There are varied *personnel supervisors* and *assistant personnel directors* in charge of the several different divisions of the personnel department. The number and types of personnel workers vary with the size and nature of the individual business enterprise, government agency or other organization. The *personnel manager,* also known as the *personnel director,* supervises the activities of all the personnel workers and is in charge of the over-all functioning of the personnel department.

A college degree with major preferably in personnel administration, industrial psychology or business administration is necessary for entry into this field. Those who hope to advance to supervisory and management positions should have the master's degree.

NONTRADITIONAL CAREERS FOR WOMEN

The employment outlook appears to be favorable in the non-traditional jobs for women in the field of personnel administration, especially for those who have graduate training in recruitment, interviewing and psychological testing. Further information about careers in personnel administration is available from the American Society for Personnel Administration, 19 Church St., Berea, Ohio 44017.

Few women have reached the top as personnel managers of large business organizations. To do so takes above-average intelligence, tact, patience, exceptional ability to speak effectively and relate well with people of all levels and a pleasing, persuasive personality; in totality, it takes a truly outstanding woman. Such a woman is Wilma C. Rogalin, who for a number of years was Personnel Manager at Pan American World Airways. In January, 1973, she was promoted to the position of Senior Manager, Women's Opportunities.

"After completing college," says Ms. Rogalin, "I decided to enter the personnel field. My undergraduate degree was a bachelor of science in social service from the University of Minnesota, and later I received my master's degree in personnel at Columbia University by taking courses at night while working for Pan American World Airways. The fields of social service and personnel are related. My interest in personnel stemmed from my enjoyment in working with people and the fact that personnel work deals with people and being of assistance to them. The phases of personnel work have expanded from interviewing, placement, benefits, counseling and job evaluation to include the handling of grievances, collective bargaining negotiations with unions, consideration of minorities and women's rights and related specialized activities.

"Prior to becoming Manager of Personnel for the Executive Offices of Pan Am in New York City, I functioned as Administrative Assistant to Pan Am's Vice-President of Industrial Relations. We were involved in labor negotiations of many groups, including pilots, clerks, mechanics, flight service personnel and flight engineers. In addition to negotiations, we were involved in arbitrations, mediations, boards of adjustment, salary and job evaluation programs, benefits, interpretations of administrative policies and union agreements and other related activities."

Ms. Rogalin adds: "When the new position of Personnel Manager of the Executive Offices was established, I was selected by my superiors, who had worked with me in the personnel and labor fields mentioned above. Apparently I was appointed not only because of my experience within the field, but also because I had secured my master's degree in personnel."

"For the past many years, my personnel department at Pan Am has serviced over 3,000 employees," states Ms. Rogalin. "We interview applicants, fill job requests, keep records and process compensation, handle union grievances and work with union representatives, acknowledge and answer correspondence, administer the various benefits, including hospital plans, life and accident insurance, disability insurance, workmen's compensation and dental and visual insurance. We coordinate such activities as charity drives, blood banks and employee social activities. We counsel department supervisors and employees on all phases of personnel activities within the company and work with union representatives who represent approximately half of our employees. The work is especially gratifying since it deals with people, and it is always stimulating as no one day is the same as another."

"Women are particularly suited for administration which is involved in personnel work," Ms. Rogalin contends. "For students interested in people and also in being of service," she says, "I suggest courses in management, psychology, writing, speaking, in addition to a personnel curriculum as a preparation for the personnel field. Personnel work opens the door to familiarity with the functioning of a company, its employees and the functioning of the various positions."

In the past two decades, air transportation has developed very

177

rapidly. Approximately half a million *aviation workers* were employed in a variety of positions in the civil aviation industry in 1970. In addition to the secretarial and related personnel, many of these workers were *reservation clerks, ticket agents* and *traffic agents,* occupations which are either female-dominated or which women have had little difficulty entering. Those who wish further information about these occupations should write to the Air Line Employees Association, International, 5600 S. Central Ave., Chicago, Ill. 60638.

The traditional female occupation in aviation is that of the *airline stewardess.* There were approximately 35,000 airline stewardesses working for scheduled airlines in 1970. Despite keen competition, employment prospects in this so-called glamorous occupation are very favorable because of the anticipated increases in air travel. Since this is traditionally a "woman's occupation," we will not go into further detail here. For additional information, write to the Stewardess Branch, Air Line Pilots Association, 1329 E St. N.W., Washington, D.C. 20004.

Pilots and *copilots, flight engineers, aircraft mechanics* (see the "mechanics" section in Chapter 10), *airline dispatchers* and *ground radio operators and teletypists* are male-dominated aviation occupations. More than 27,000 pilots and copilots and approximately 8,500 flight engineers were employed by the scheduled airlines in 1970; all were licensed by the Federal Aviation Administration. There were also about 1,200 airline dispatchers and assistant dispatchers and about 7,000 ground radio operators and teletypists at work in air transporation in 1970. All of these have been all-male occupations. It will not be easy for women to enter these occupations, but those who are determined to do so should get all of the necessary training and preparation, plus much more.

For further information about these aviation careers, write to the Air Line Pilots Association, 1329 E St. N.W., Washington, D.C. 20004; the Flight Engineers International Association, 100

Indiana Ave. N.W., Washington, D.C. 20001; and/or the Air Line Dispatchers Association, 929 W. Broad St., Falls Church, Va. 22130.

Wilma C. Rogalin of Pan Am has some pertinent comments concerning these specialized positions. She says, "In the airlines, as in many fields, women are breaking through into various areas. As officers and department heads, they are obtaining top administrative experience. They have been welcomed into the legal, data-processing and operations' fields. Until women in greater numbers are qualified in specialized fields such as engineering or flying, there will not be a breakthrough in over-all job opportunities in various specialized fields."

The Federal Aviation Administration (FAA) of the U.S. Department of Transportation employs specialized aviation personnel to enable it to conduct its regulatory functions. Within the FAA, there are four major occupational areas where men have predominated—namely, air traffic control, electronic technician work, engineering (especially aerospace, civil and electronic) and flight standards inspection. As of April 30, 1972, there were in the FAA 24,665 *air traffic controllers*, of whom 339 were women; 8,934 *electronic technicians*, of whom only ten were women; 2,433 *engineers*, of whom twenty-one were women; and 2,160 *flight standards inspectors*, of whom only six were women.

Efforts are being made to recruit women into these occupations. The most rapid progress in female recruitment will probably be made among the air traffic controllers and electronic technicians, since these two positions do not call for as rigid educational and experience requirements as the other two occupations do. Special programs have been in operation since February, 1970, at the FAA Academy to aid in the recruitment and training of women and members of minorities. If you would like further information about these programs, write to the Director of Civil Rights, Federal Aviation Administration, U.S. Department of Transportation, Washington, D.C. 20591.

NONTRADITIONAL CAREERS FOR WOMEN

Since aviation transportation is growing rapidly and providing increasing employment opportunities for thousands of miscellaneous personnel, there are those who think railroad transportation is vanishing. This is far from true; the railroads are still very much alive and will continue to be so. More than 500,000 *railroad workers* were employed in 1970. The male-dominated occupations of the *brakemen, conductors, locomotive engineers* and *locomotive firemen* have declined in size in recent years, but increasing opportunities in railroading are becoming available to women in management positions. The data-processing area of railroad administration is opening up many opportunities to women. If you would like to learn more about career opportunities for women in railroading, write to Cynthia Y. Soltes, President, American Council of Railroad Women, c/o Illinois Central Railroad Co., 135 E. 11th Place, 600 Annex, Chicago, Ill. 60605, and/or the Association of American Railroads, 1920 L St. N.W., Washington, D.C. 20036.

The driving occupations are an important part of the transportation industry. The number of women *bus drivers* and *taxi drivers* is small. The number of women *truck drivers* is even smaller. In large cities, increasing numbers of women are finding employment as bus drivers and taxi drivers, especially the latter. There are expanding opportunities for women as independent taxi owners. Although women are being hired as truck drivers and some trucking companies are hiring husband-and-wife "truck driver teams," the number of women truck drivers will probably remain small for quite some time. For further information about careers in trucking, write to the American Trucking Association, Inc., 1616 P St. N.W., Washington, D.C. 20036.

Many opportunities are becoming available to qualified female college graduates in the management and administrative aspects of transportation, several of which we have already noted. If you would like further information, write to the American Society of

Traffic and Transportation, Inc., 547 W. Jackson Blvd., Chicago, Ill. 60606.

The travel agency branch of the transportation industry is presenting new and growing opportunities to women as *travel agents* and as *travel agency owners*. Write to the American Society of Travel Agents, Education and Training Department, 360 Lexington Ave., New York, N.Y. 10017, if you are interested in further details about these careers.

The hotel business plays an important role in the lives of those who travel. Women constitute approximately 50 per cent of the employees in hotels and related businesses, but they are only a small percentage of the *assistant hotel managers, hotel managers* and *motel managers*. In 1970, there were more than 190,000 hotel and motel managers throughout the nation; approximately 90,000 were salaried employees, and the remainder were owner-managers.

Hotel experience, especially in front-office jobs, is necessary for advancement to assistant hotel manager and hotel or motel manager positions. Additionally, graduation from a college offering a four-year curriculum in hotel and motel administration is desirable. The courses offered by the Educational Institute of the American Hotel and Motel Association are very valuable too. The outlook is bright for the college-educated woman who aspires to a hotel management career and who has a pleasant personality, a ready smile and genuine concern for the welfare of the guests and has completed appropriate hotel administration courses.

If you would like additional information about careers and training programs in hotel and motel management, write to the American Hotel and Motel Association, 888 Seventh Ave., New York, N.Y. 10019, and the Educational Institute of the American Hotel and Motel Association, 77 Kellogg Center, East Lansing, Mich. 48823.

The largest group of professional workers in the field of business administration consists of the *accountants*. There were approximately 500,000 accountants at work in the United States in 1970. About one-fifth of them were *certified public accountants (CPAs)*. Women represent about 20 per cent of the total number of accountants and less than 3 per cent of the CPAs.

Accountants design new systems or modify existing systems of keeping the records of a business establishment's assets, liabilities and financial transactions. They compile and analyze these records and prepare miscellaneous financial reports. Some accountants specialize in tax problems and preparing tax returns and are known as *tax accountants*. Others specialize in auditing; they examine and review accounting records and prepare reports on their employer's financial status and operating procedures. They are known as *auditors*.

The bachelor's degree with major study in accounting is the desirable minimum requirement to qualify as an accountant. There are a number of ways to prepare for this profession. You may take accounting courses in the day or evening sessions of universities, four-year colleges or two-year community or junior colleges, or you may attend approved private business schools. Those who wish to advance in the business world should obtain a master's degree in accounting or business administration.

Accountants should have an analytical mind, numerical aptitude, organizational ability and an interest in business and finance. They should be painstakingly accurate and patient and pleasant with their clients. Accountants are employed by all types of business, industrial and governmental organizations. Many work for the federal government as Internal Revenue agents (see Chapter 11). Many others are self-employed and are engaged in public accounting as proprietors or partners.

The letters "CPA" after an accountant's name indicate that she is a *certified public accountant*. This means that the accountant has satisfied the educational and experience requirements, passed the CPA examination which is administered by the American Institute of Certified Public Accountants and been awarded the CPA certificate by her state board of accountancy. The first woman CPA was awarded her certificate in 1899. In 1972, there were about 2,800 women CPAs.

There are excellent opportunities for women in the field of accounting. During the remainder of the 1970s, employment is expected to expand very rapidly in this field. Women who like the world of business and enjoy working with numbers and people should find accounting very attractive.

In past years, women were the bookkeepers and men were the accountants. Now the doors are opening to you and you too can become an accountant if you wish. You could establish an independent practice at home and arrange your working hours to comply with your home and family obligations. The need for accountants is so great that if your husband's work makes it necessary for you to relocate, you would have little, if any, difficulty finding employment in your new setting.

Women accountants have two professional associations of their own. There are the American Society of Women Accountants and the American Woman's Society of Certified Public Accountants. Both have their national headquarters at 327 S. LaSalle St., Chicago, Ill. 60604. You may write to either one or both for further information about career opportunities for women in accounting.

If you wish to obtain additional information about accounting careers, you may also write to the American Institute of Certified Public Accountants, 666 Fifth Ave., New York, N.Y. 10019, and/or the National Association of Accountants, 505 Park Ave., New York, N.Y. 10022.

Also involved in finance are, of course, the *bank personnel.* Banking is a service business, and banks provide such a variety of services to their customers that they are sometimes called "department stores of finance." The vast majority of bank personnel are *bank clerks* and *bank tellers.*

NONTRADITIONAL CAREERS FOR WOMEN

Over 500,000 clerical employees worked in banks throughout the nation in 1970, and approximately 90 per cent of them were women. There were also about 230,000 *bank tellers,* of whom again about 90 per cent were women. A very rapid increase is expected in employment opportunities for tellers as banks increase the number of their branches and expand their services. Although women predominate as clerks and tellers, they represent only 14 per cent of the estimated 175,000 *bank officers.*

High school graduation is sufficient for positions as bank clerks and bank tellers. College graduation with a major in finance or business administration, however, is required for entrance into any bank management trainee programs. Qualified candidates are selected for officer-training programs, which range from six months to one year in length. Now that discrimination on the basis of sex is against the law, if you have the necessary training, qualifications and bank experience, the outlook for your advancement to bank officer positions appears much more favorable than ever before. Banks are everywhere, and they are expanding. Thus, it is expected that the number of bank officers will increase rapidly during the remainder of the 1970s. With this should come increasing opportunities for upward mobility for women into the ranks of management.

In 1921, six women who held important positions in New York City banks founded the National Association of Bank-Women. Members must hold officer status in a bank. Today NABW has over 10,000 members from all of the fifty states, and they represent all aspects of banking, such as branch management, computer operations, investments, loans, personnel, public relations and trusts. For further information, write to the National Association of Bank-Women, Inc., 111 E. Wacker Drive, Chicago, Ill. 60601. If you would like additional information about careers in banking, write to the American Bankers Association, 1120 Connecticut Ave. N.W., Washington, D.C. 20036.

Computer operations and the new techniques for processing

business data are, as you have just learned, important in the administrative aspects of banking, the railroad industry and aviation. The field of electronic data processing is making thousands of employment opportunities available to many people, not just in the three aforementioned industries but also in a great many more places.

In the 1960s, computers began proving their great value to the business, educational and scientific worlds, and they were put to use in ever-increasing numbers. There are now more than 60,000 functioning computers throughout the nation, and this number will grow rapidly as time goes on. Some people call the electronic computer a "mechanical brain." However, it is not really a "brain" for it cannot think for itself. It can only follow the step-by-step instructions fed to it by human beings.

Electronic computer operating personnel include the many specialized operators who are required to enable the computer to perform the functions for which it was created, from information (data) processing to doing very complex computations. Computers can store large amounts of data for use at some future date and also do complex mathematical calculations at fantastic speeds. The number and kinds of personnel needed to operate a computer vary according to the type and size of the computer. In 1972, there were more than 200,000 persons employed as *console and auxiliary equipment operators. Computer operators,* also known as *console operators,* ready the equipment for the "run" by adjusting the various dials and switches and inserting the necessary tapes, discs or cards; the latter are the punched cards prepared by the *keypunch operator.*

Computer programmers analyze the facts and figures to be processed or the problems to be solved and prepare the step-by-step instructions to guide the computer operator. There were about 200,000 programmers at work in the United States in 1972; these were the programmers employed by business establishments and government agencies, and did not include the engineers, scientists, mathematicians and others who did programming in the scientific and educational worlds. Although women in increasing numbers have begun to become computer programmers, the majority of programmers are men.

Systems analysts analyze miscellaneous business problems and convert them into programmable form for application to an electronic data-processing system. They develop systems which process data in order to solve business, scientific or engineering problems. In the business world, they plan, schedule and coordinate the activities needed to develop systems involved in the solution of such problems as inventory control and cost analysis. There were over 100,000 systems analysts at work in 1972; very few of them were women.

There are many different types of jobs in the field of electronic data processing (EDP), and educational requirements vary with the nature of each position. High school graduation may be sufficient for many of the console and auxiliary equipment operators, including the key-punch operators; on-the-job training, during which they are taught how to perform many data-processing functions, is often available to capable high school graduates. The completion of at least a two-year EDP program in a community or junior college is desirable for computer programmers.

There is no standard prescribed program of required preparation for becoming a systems analyst. A bachelor's degree with major in computer science or data processing is desirable, although major study in accounting or business administration is also acceptable. A good background in engineering, mathematics and science is necessary for those who will be working for engineering companies. (For information about computer engineers, see Chapter 7.) Some employers have begun to stress the importance of graduate study for appointment to positions as systems analysts; almost all require that the candidates for such positions have experience as computer programmers.

Computer operating personnel should have mechanical aptitude and finger dexterity for the competent operation of the EDP equipment and should have the ability to reason logically. Computer programmers and systems analysts should possess a logical mind, the ability to accurately analyze and work with data, the patience to pay close attention to detail and the capacity to solve problems in an orderly fashion.

Employment opportunities should be excellent throughout the 1970s for persons trained and qualified to work in the field of electronic data processing. It is anticipated that there will be a rapid expansion of computer installations and a growing demand for electronic data-processing systems in business and government, and with these should come a very rapid growth in employment of electronic computer operating personnel, programmers and systems analysts. Do you have a logical, detail-seeking mind? Women with such minds are needed in these new, expanding EDP occupations.

If you would like further information about careers in EDP, write to the American Federation of Information Processing Societies, 210 Summit Ave., Montvale, N.J. 07645, and/or the Data Processing Management Association, 505 Busse Highway, Park Ridge, Ill. 60068.

The wheels of business would come to an unhappy halt if there were no *salespeople* to sell to the public the vast variety of products and services produced by the manufacturing firms and other business enterprises of our country and imported from foreign countries. There were over 5,000,000 persons working in the sales occupations in 1972. Forty per cent of these salespeople were women, and they were concentrated in retail sales. In all sales fields other than retail, such as insurance, real estate and wholesale trade, men predominate.

More than 52 per cent of all the salespeople work in retail trade. There were nearly 3,000,000 *retail salespeople* at work throughout the United States in 1972, and about 60 per cent of them were *retail saleswomen*.

Retail selling is traditionally a woman's occupation, and so we

187

shall not go into further detail about this occupation here. However, it should be noted that whereas retail saleswomen outnumber men in department stores, drugstores, general merchandise and variety stores and apparel and accessories shops, retail salesmen predominate in the selling of automobiles, farm equipment, furniture, hardware, lumber and shoes.

Furniture salespeople must be capable of answering questions about the construction of selected pieces. To sell expensive or specialized items, you must be well versed in the characteristics, construction and operation of these items. Thus, as a retail saleswoman, if you would like to sell products generally sold by men, you should become very knowledgeable about these products; then apply to the head of that particular department and do a good job of convincing him of your capabilities.

Prospects for employment are good for full-time and part-time retail salespeople. For further information about careers in retail sales, write to the National Retail Merchants Association, 100 W. 31st St., New York, N.Y. 10001.

Automobile salespeople are the link between the automobile dealer and the automobile buyer. Most sell only new cars; some sell only used cars; and others sell both new and used cars. The exact number of *automobile saleswomen* is unknown, but it is known that they represent a tiny percentage of the presently estimated 120,000 automobile salespeople.

The minimum educational requirement for automobile salespeople is a high school diploma. Beginners are often trained on the job. Are you capable of driving a car? Are you well versed in all aspects of the operation of an automobile? Are you tactful, persuasive, well groomed and capable of expressing yourself well? If you are, then perhaps you should aim to become an automobile saleswoman and perhaps even aim someday to have your own dealership.

It is anticipated that the number of automobile salespeople will increase moderately throughout the 1970s as car sales rise with national growth in population and multicar ownership. If you would like more information about careers in automobile selling and dealerships, write to the National Automobile Dealers Association, 2000 K St. N.W., Washington, D.C. 20006.

A small but steadily increasing number of women are being hired as *automobile parts counterwomen.* The estimated 68,000 salespeople who sold automobile parts over the counter in 1970 worked mostly for automobile dealers and parts wholesalers. The employment outlook for women is especially bright here as more women are being employed as counter personnel by dealers and in the jobbing stores. More details about careers as automobile parts counterwomen may be obtained by writing to the National Automotive Parts Association, 10400 W. Higgins Road, Rosemont, Ill. 60018.

Gasoline service station attendants, also known as *automobile service station salespeople,* service cars and other automotive vehicles with fuel, lubricants and accessories. They may perform a number of other varied services, from cleaning the windshield to giving street directions to making minor repairs. Approximately 410,000 service station attendants were at work in 1970, and about one-third worked part-time; a very small number of women were attendants.

There is no reason why women who can drive a car, are persuasive and have mechanical aptitude could not be competent gasoline service station attendants. The growing consumption of gasoline should bring with it a rise in employment opportunities for women in this occupation; the many part-time opportunities should be especially attractive to women. Inquire at your local gasoline service stations for work possibilities. Perhaps you may even decide someday to own your own gasoline station.

Wholesale salespeople work for wholesalers and bring the products from the factories where they were manufactured to the retail stores where they are purchased by the public. There were approximately 550,000 salespeople working for wholesalers in

1972, and only a small percentage of them were women. Salespeople in wholesale trade pay periodic calls on the retailers in their prescribed "territory." They show these retailers the latest catalogues of the products handled by their wholesaler-employers and aim to convince them to purchase these products. Women who work indoors in retail establishments may wish to go outdoors and sell to retailers rather than directly to the public.

A college education is desirable for wholesale salespeople, particularly when they handle a line of technical products, in contrast to the high school education which is sufficient for retail salespeople. Women who have sales ability, a good deal of self-confidence and a pleasant personality should find good opportunities available to them as saleswomen in wholesale trade as business activity increases throughout the 1970s. For further information, write to the National Association of Wholesalers-Distributors, 1725 K St. N.W., Washington, D.C. 20006.

In addition to the salespeople who work for wholesalers, there are those who work for the manufacturers themselves. These *manufacturers' salespeople,* also known as *manufacturers' sales representatives,* generally sell their employers' products to other businesses, which in turn eventually get these products to the consumer. Those who work for manufacturers of highly technical and scientific products are often called *sales engineers.*

Of somewhat more than 500,000 manufacturers' salespeople at work in 1970, approximately 10 per cent were women and most of them were employed by manufacturers of food products. Although high school education is generally considered adequate preparation for this occupation, college training is becoming advisable. Persuasive women who have their college education, especially those who are knowledgeable about food and technical products, should find a favorable employment future as manufacturers' representatives. If this occupation appeals to you, write directly to the manufacturer for whom you would like to work.

Securities salespeople execute the buying or selling transactions for investors who wish to purchase or sell stocks, bonds or other securities. These salespeople are also called *customers' brokers*. There were approximately 200,000 of these brokers at work in 1970, and more than one-third of them worked part-time. The exact number of women in this occupation is not known, but the great majority of securities salespeople are men.

A bachelor's degree with a major in business administration, including courses in finance and the securities business, is desirable. Securities salespeople are required to be licensed in almost all states. Most brokerage firms, investment bankers and mutual fund firms have special training programs to help their trainees meet the licensure requirements; these programs are at least six months in length and often longer.

This occupation should be very attractive to women who are interested in finance, like to work directly with people and are able to speak well and in a convincing manner. Securities salespeople may arrange to see their customers in their homes in the evenings or on weekends and may work on a part-time basis. These working conditions enable women customers' brokers to combine careers with home and family commitments. Employment opportunities for women as brokers appear to be good for the years ahead.

If you are interested in further information about the securities business, write to the New York Stock Exchange, 11 Wall St., New York, N.Y. 10005, and/or the National Association of Securities Dealers, Inc., 1735 K St. N.W., Washington, D.C. 20006.

The real estate and insurance industries also offer many thousands of employment opportunities for salespeople and for others too. *Real estate brokers* are independent businessmen who seek buyers for real estate which the property owners have asked them to sell. They may also arrange for loans to finance the purchases of property, rent and manage properties, make appraisals and perform a miscellany of other related real estate

191

functions. *Real estate salespeople* work for brokers and help them to sell the property which the brokers' clients have put up for sale. Real estate brokers and real estate salespeople are both also called *real estate agents*. Agents who are members of the National Association of Real Estate Boards may carry the title *"realtor."*

The minimum educational requirement for beginner's positions in this field is the high school diploma. Many community colleges offer real estate courses, and the associate degree with a major in real estate is becoming desirable. There are also now many real estate agents who are college graduates. Every state and the District of Columbia require that real estate salespeople and brokers be licensed. This involves passing a written examination; the examination for brokers is much more comprehensive than the one for salespeople.

The field of real estate selling has a tremendous number of part-time workers. In 1972, there were about a million agents licensed to sell real estate. It is estimated that only about one-fourth of them were working at this occupation full-time; the vast remainder were part-timers. Of the estimated 250,000 full-time real estate agents, about 40 per cent were women.

There are very good opportunities as real estate agents for women who are mature, intelligent and tactful and have a good memory, pleasant personality and dignified appearance. Those who wish may work part-time. Women who become licensed brokers may open their own offices and go into business for themselves. For more details about careers in real estate, write to the National Association of Real Estate Boards, 155 E. Superior St., Chicago, Ill. 60611.

In the insurance field, the terms "salesperson," "agent" and "broker" are often used interchangeably and synonymously. The *insurance agents* and *insurance brokers* are *insurance salespeople*. However, whereas insurance agents are either employees of one specific insurance company or under contract to serve as the authorized representatives of one or more companies and sell policies for these companies, insurance brokers work either for themselves or for brokerage firms and sell insurance for many different companies. The brokers are not under contract to any insurance company, and they place the policies they sell with the companies which best satisfy their customers' needs. Thus, the agents, actually, directly represent the insurance companies, whereas the brokers directly represent the policyholders.

Basically, agents and brokers do similar work; they sell insurance, collect payments (premiums) from policyholders, help policyholders to settle claims and attend to changes and renewals in coverage. There were about 350,000 full-time agents and brokers engaged in the sale of insurance in 1970. About another 150,000 worked on a part-time basis. Only 10 per cent of the total number of these insurance agents and brokers were women.

Some insurance companies hire intelligent, personable high school graduates as *agent-trainees*, but applicants who have a bachelor's degree with a major in economics, finance or business administration are given preference. All agents must be licensed by the states in which they plan to sell insurance. After the agent-trainee has successfully completed the training program, the employing company may sponsor this beginner's license application. In most states, applicants must pass a written examination before they are awarded their license.

Life, property and liability and health insurance are the three basic types of insurance and all of these are matters which should concern women. This type of selling, especially on a part-time basis, should appeal to women who are interested in insurance and in helping potential policyholders in planning the financial protection which best meets their special needs. The abilities to inspire confidence in others, to explain clearly the nature of different policies and to listen patiently to policyholders' questions and answer them lucidly are important assets. The outlook is favorable for women who have these assets despite the fact that insurance selling is keenly competitive.

NONTRADITIONAL CAREERS FOR WOMEN

The insurance business is vital to all other businesses, for it provides protection and, thereby, security to individuals, groups, families and businesses. Insurance, like banking, is a service business. There are approximately 1,500,000 people employed in the insurance business, and the vast majority are clerical workers and salespeople. In addition to the latter, which we have already discussed, there are the traditionally male-dominated occupations of the *claims adjusters* and the *underwriters.*

Claims adjusters investigate, negotiate and try to settle out of court claims for loss or damages filed in conjunction with an insurance policy. There were approximately 114,000 claim adjusters in 1970, and most of them were men. There are no standard educational requirements for claim adjusting, but the trend is toward the hiring of college graduates.

Underwriters review individual applications for insurance to determine the degree of risk involved and decide upon the risks their companies will insure. Most of the 55,000 underwriters employed in 1970 were men. The bachelor's degree, preferably with a major in business administration, is desirable for the entry-level positions as *underwriting trainees* or *junior underwriters.*

Whereas claims adjusters should enjoy working with people because their work keeps them on the go and brings them into contact with claimants, witnesses, policyholders and others, underwriters have sedentary jobs and must spend their time patiently evaluating facts and figures. The employment outlook for women as claims adjusters and underwriters is favorable if they have the necessary personality characteristics and acquire the desirable training and experience.

The National Association of Insurance Women was founded in 1940. Today N.A.I.W. has more than 15,000 members, and they hold a variety of positions in the insurance business. In 1969, N.A.I.W. started its program of professional designation, C.P.I.W. The letters "CPIW" stand for "Certified Professional Insurance Woman." A C.P.I.W. certificate is awarded to those women who

194

meet the prescribed experience, education and length of membership requirements. If you would like additional information, write to the National Association of Insurance Women, International, 1847 E. 15th St., Tulsa, Okla. 74104.

For further details about careers in insurance, write to any or all of the following: National Association of Insurance Agents, Inc., 96 Fulton St., New York, N.Y. 10038; Institute of Life Insurance, 277 Park Ave., New York, N.Y. 10017; and Insurance Information Institute, 110 William St., New York, N.Y. 10038. For information about education preparation, write to the College of Insurance, 150 William St., New York, N.Y. 10038.

Whether salespeople sell services or products, they depend a great deal on the advertising business to help them do their selling. Advertising aims to increase the sales of the advertised products and services by bringing them to the attention of the public. The advertisement you see in the newspapers and/or magazines and the commercial you hear and/or see on the radio and television are the results of the combined efforts of many *advertising workers* who possess diverse talents and dissimilar backgrounds.

A large business concern may have its own advertising department headed by an *advertising manager*, who directs this company's advertising program. This advertising manager may decide to use the services of an advertising agency; if so, the manager works with the *account executive* of the advertising agency to plan the most appropriate advertising campaign for this company.

The *copywriters* then write the words (the "copy"—the headlines, slogans and text) which become part of the advertisements or commercials and are aimed to catch the readers' or viewers' attention. The *layout artists* and *advertising artists* (see Chapter 8) prepare the art work. The *production workers* convert the completed copy and art work into the finished advertisement or commercial in either printed or filmed form.

NONTRADITIONAL CAREERS FOR WOMEN

Media directors decide which media—newspapers, magazines, radio, television stations or other carriers of advertising—are best for their ads—namely, which will help them reach the largest number of potential purchasers of their products or services at the least cost to their company. *Space buyers* and *time buyers* then buy the desired amount of space for their advertisement to appear on a specified day in a specific newspaper or magazine or a certain amount of time on the radio or television station on which they want their commercial to be presented; they buy this space and time from the *space sellers* and *time sellers* of the respective media.

Market research workers are members of a team which conducts surveys to try to find out what the public likes and dislikes and why. The information they uncover may result in changes in their company's products and/or services and will influence the course of their company's future advertising campaigns. Miscellaneous *public relations workers,* including *press agents, promotion managers, public relations women* and *publicity directors,* are involved in planning, directing and carrying out public relations programs to promote favorable publicity, create good will and present a positive public image for their employers.

The educational requirements for entry into these fields vary with each particular occupation and range from the necessity for a high school diploma and creative talent for the artists to the desirability of a master's degree, with a major in advertising or business administration, for the account executives and department managers. For all advertising, market research and public relations workers, the ability to come up with new ideas, to work under pressure and to express oneself simply and lucidly is most desirable.

Talented women who possess this ability, plus drive, initiative, organizational ability and a knowledge of the business world, should find a bright employment outlook for them in these fields. Some exceptionally talented women may even start their own advertising agencies. Joan Murray, the noted TV news correspondent, who cofounded ZEBRA Associates, the nation's largest black-owned advertising agency, is such a woman. (Read what she has to say in Chapter 8.)

Advertising, market research and public relations have been male-dominated fields. However, women recently have begun to make inroads into them; this is especially true in the public relations field, which women have been entering in ever-increasing numbers.

For further career information and lists of schools which offer training in these fields, write to one or more of the following according to your individual interests: American Advertising Federation, 1225 Connecticut Ave. N.W., Washington, D.C. 20036; American Association of Advertising Agencies, 200 Park Ave., New York, N.Y. 10017; American Marketing Association, 230 N. Michigan Ave., Chicago, Ill. 60601; and Public Relations Society of America, Inc., 845 Third Ave., New York, N.Y. 10022.

All of the women in the business world play a role, be it little or big, in making the wheels of business turn; but none with such power as the women at the top of the corporate ladder—the managers and the executives. We have already mentioned several of these *departmental managers*.

Business enterprises may succeed or fail depending on how well *business managers*—on all levels—do their jobs. *Manager-trainees, administrative assistants, junior executives* and *supervisors* hold entry-level management positions. The *middle-level managers* are next, and they generally head the large, important departments within the company; they include the *personnel managers, production managers, purchasing managers* and *sales managers*. The *top-level managers* include the *corporation presidents, vice-presidents* and other *corporate executives*, who meet to make the major decisions which set the company's policies.

Over 6,000,000 salaried workers were employed in managerial occupations in 1970. About 15 per cent (about 900,000) were women. Additionally, about 2,200,000 persons were *self-employed business proprietors* who managed all or part of their own businesses, and an estimated 25 per cent of them were women.

Women have long found it difficult and, in some corporations, sometimes impossible to get their toes onto the rungs of the managerial ladder. The vast majority of women in managerial positions have been in entry-level posts. But, fortunately, times are changing and the number of middle-level managers is increasing. There has always been very little room at the very top for women, but the number of women on the uppermost rungs of the corporate ladder will increase, albeit slowly, as times goes on. Women who become corporate executives are generally college-educated women, often with more than one degree, of exceptional wisdom, maturity, judgment and leadership ability.

If you would like to become a manager of your own business, it is advisable that you first acquire experience working for someone else in the field in which you would like to become self-employed. Tremendous satisfaction and a feeling of independence come from being one's own boss. Many of the professions and other occupations included in this book offer you the opportunity to become self-employed. Aside from these, women who want to be self-employed are most apt to become proprietors of retail or service establishments.

Before you go into business for yourself, there are many factors you must consider, such as the amount of capital needed, from whom you will get additional capital if needed, where to locate your business, the laws and regulations which will affect you as a business owner, the prices to charge and how to keep the records of your business transactions. Additionally, you should be energetic, industrious, not easily discouraged, capable of self-discipline and willing to work hard for long hours if necessary and have initiative, above-average sales ability, good organizing ability and a sense of responsibility.

Entering into your own business and becoming self-employed involves certain risks. You can reduce these risks by consulting a competent lawyer, accountant, the local banker and representatives from your local Better Business Bureau, your local Chamber of Commerce, your Trade Association and the nearest office of the United States Small Business Administration.

The Small Business Administration publishes an excellent "Starting and Managing Series" of pamphlets which are chockfull of valuable information. Among the recent titles in this series is *Starting and Managing a Small Drive-In Restaurant*, which is available for thirty-five cents from the U.S. Government Printing Office, Washington, D.C. 20402; it explains the drive-in restaurant business, what it takes to succeed, financing, choosing a location, the building and equipment, legal matters, management controls, personnel management, record keeping, advertising and promotion and franchising.

Additionally, the Small Business Administration publishes "Small Marketers Aids," "Management Aids for Small Manufacturers" and other helpful materials. For information about their publications and other services, write to the U.S. Small Business Administration, Washington, D.C. 20416.

Our great democratic system of free enterprise enables you to become self-employed and your dreams to become realities. If you have some good ideas and want to go into business and become your own boss, acquire the necessary preliminary knowledge, experience, advice, training and capital and go to it, and may your enterprise be a resounding success!

Women in the business world should be interested in the American Business Women's Association. The American Business Women's Association is an educational association which was founded in September, 1949. It has over 1,000 chapters and more than 60,000 members throughout the fifty states. The major aims of A.B.W.A. are "the improvement of employer-employee relations, keeping business women up to date on business techniques and advancing women in business through more efficient service to business. For further information, write to the American Business Women's Association, 9100 Ward Parkway, Kansas City, Mo. 64114.

Chapter 10

WOMEN IN
MANUAL TRADES

YOU have already learned from earlier sections of this book that there are certain occupations which have traditionally been perceived as "feminine" and others as "masculine." Nowhere, however, have these sexist prejudices been as strong as in the manual trades.

Whereas many other traditionally male occupations have begun to yield and give women a warm welcome, the manual trades would apparently prefer to freeze females out rather than welcome them in.

As I stated at the start of this book, to make this book as comprehensive, up-to-date and accurate as possible, I sent out hundreds of questionnaires to professional associations, labor unions, women's organizations, government agencies, educational institutions and a miscellany of other groups in any way involved with employment opportunities for women. The response was very good from all groups *except* the labor unions representing the skilled trades! In some cases, even follow-up letters, phone calls and personal communications brought forth little if any response, and this little response was often rather meaningless and worthless.

Federal law now prohibits discrimination on the basis of sex. Thus, no employer or company may say he will not hire a woman if she is qualified for the job. But, in the manual trades, one cannot help getting the impression that the labor unions and the employers are hoping that the women will go away and, preferably, go back to the kitchen.

One labor union official said to me, "Lady, these are *man*ual trades." He repeated, with even greater emphasis, "*MAN*ual trades—you know what that means—it means it's work for a MAN, not for a lady!"

A Women's Libber, to whom I told this little tale, said, "I would have told him, we're going to make them 'WOMANual' trades."

Well, these occupations are neither MANual, as the labor union official said, nor WOMANual, as the Women's Libber hopes they will become. Actually, the "man" in the word "manual" is derived from the Latin word *manus,* which means "hand," and these occupations call for skill with one's hands, or what is technically called manual dexterity.

Manual dexterity is not something exclusive to members of the male sex. There are many, many women who have above-average manual dexterity and many, many men who do not. Most of the manual trades require eye-hand coordination, in addition to finger and hand dexterity, and this, too, many women possess. Those who defend sexist discrimination in the skilled trades often say they do so because a great deal of physical strength is needed to work in these trades. This is not true. In many of these occupations, it is generally not necessary to lift more than twenty pounds, and most frequently it is unnecessary to lift more than half that weight.

Exact figures are unavailable, but it has been estimated that in many of the manual occupations as little as 1 per cent, or even less, of the members of these occupations are women. There are serious manpower shortages in many of these trades, and womanpower is needed to ease these shortages. Workers in the skilled trades are often called *craftsmen.*

NONTRADITIONAL CAREERS FOR WOMEN

Rapid increases in employment opportunities are anticipated in many of these trades. Among the latter are the following occupations in the building trades: *bricklayers,* who use bricks and other masonry materials to build houses, walls, chimneys, fireplaces, partitions and varied other structures; *carpenters,* who constitute the largest single group of skilled workers and perform a multitude of jobs in either "rough" and/or "finish" carpentry; *cement masons,* who finish the exposed concrete surfaces on such areas as floors, sidewalks, walls, highways and airport runways; *construction electricians,* who install, test and repair electrical fixtures, apparatus and wiring used in electrical systems; *floor covering installers,* who install, replace and repair a variety of floor coverings; *glaziers,* who cut, fit and install plate glass, ordinary window glass, mirrors and other special glass items; and *lathers,* who install the support backings on which plaster, stucco or concrete materials are applied.

Also among them are the *operating engineers,* also known as *construction machinery operators,* who operate, maintain and repair power-driven construction machinery; *painters* and *paperhangers,* who prepare surfaces for painting or papering, respectively, and then apply coats of paint, paper strips or other materials to either interior or exterior surfaces; *plumbers* and *pipefitters,* who install pipe systems which transport water, steam, air or other liquids or gases which may be needed for health, sanitation, maintenance, industrial production or other miscellaneous purposes; *roofers,* who apply composition roofing and other materials to the roofs of buildings; and *sheet-metal workers,* who construct and install many different products made from thin sheets of metal, especially ducts used in ventilating, air-conditioning and heating systems.

Among the *mechanics* and *repairmen* for whom the employment outlook appears to be bright are the *air-conditioning, refrigeration and heating mechanics,* who work on cooling and heating equipment used in homes, offices, schools, stores and miscellaneous other buildings; *aircraft mechanics,* who overhaul, service and inspect aircraft and aircraft engines and thus keep planes operating efficiently; *appliance servicemen,* who repair the vast variety of small and large appliances found in today's homes; *automobile body repairmen,* who repair damaged motor vehicles; and *automobile mechanics,* who comprise the largest repair occupation and help to keep in good working condition the millions of automobiles, buses, trucks and similar vehicles in use throughout the United States.

Bright employment futures appear to be in the offing too for *business machine servicemen,* who maintain and repair the increasing numbers and kinds of office machines and equipment; *diesel mechanics,* who maintain and repair diesel-powered machinery and equipment, such as that used in industry and on farms and highways; *furniture upholsterers,* who install, arrange, and secure the springs, padding and various covering materials to the frames of chairs, sofas, seats and other upholstered furniture; *industrial machinery repairmen,* also known as *maintenance mechanics,* who keep in good running order the machinery and other mechanical equipment employed in a wide variety of factories; *instrument repairmen,* who repair and maintain varied complex industrial and scientific instruments; *maintenance electricians,* also called *electrical repairmen,* who work at maintaining and repairing many different kinds of electrical equipment and at modernizing this equipment in order to maintain and increase its efficiency; *television and radio service technicians,* who, in addition to television sets and radios, install and repair the burgeoning variety of electronic products, such as hi-fidelity and stereophonic sound equipment, intercommunication equipment, tape recorders and public address systems; *tool and die makers,* who produce varied tools, dies, jigs, gauges and other measuring devices, as well as the miscellaneous fixtures and special guiding and holding devices used in the mass production of ever so many items in the metalworking industries; and *watch repairmen,* also known as *watchmakers,* who clean, repair and adjust watches, clocks and varied other timepieces.

The telephone industry employed more than 100,000 *telephone and PBX installers and repairmen* and additional thousands of *central office craftsmen* and *linemen and cable splicers.* The employment outlook is favorable, and women are being hired in increasing numbers for these formerly all-male occupations.

Many skilled workers learn their crafts by attending vocational schools. Public vocational and technical schools are now accepting female students. There are also private trade and technical institutes where women can prepare for many mechanical and other manual occupations.

For information about vocational training programs in public and private schools, write to the Vocational Education Division of the State Department of Education in your state capital and request a list of the approved schools in your field of interest located in or near your community.

Many others use the apprenticeship route as their means of entry into the skilled trades. Preparation for a particular craft via the apprenticeship program is recommended by many officials in industry and the labor unions. An *apprentice* is both an employed worker and a student. An apprenticeship is an organized earn-as-you-learn program; it is a formal training program that combines progressive on-the-job training in a particular trade with related classroom instruction.

With the cooperation of the U.S. Department of Labor's Bureau of Apprenticeship and Training, the leaders of labor unions and the management of large industries have established formal apprenticeship training programs. The apprentice enters into a formal written agreement with the employer in which the conditions of the training period, length of time, amount of pay and rate of periodic increases are stated. Apprenticeships generally range from two to four years, varying according to the specific craft. The training period includes 144 hours per year of classroom instruction, given either in a local vocational school or by an instructor in the plant where the apprentice works.

Upon completion of a recognized apprenticeship program, the apprentice is awarded a Certificate of Completion of Apprenticeship and is thus certified as a *journeyman* or *craftsman.*

The exact requirements for acceptance into an apprenticeship program may differ with each craft. In the main, however, candidates for apprenticeships should be high school graduates with above-average mechanical aptitude and physical fitness for the specific apprenticeable trades of their choice. The completion of high school courses in mathematics, science and industrial or manual arts is desirable.

In 1972, women were engaged in more than sixty of over 350 skilled occupations offering apprenticeship training. Women are considered especially well suited to serve as aircraft mechanics, appliance servicewomen, automobile mechanics, business machine servicewomen, furniture upholsterers, radio and television service technicians, tool-and-die makers and watch repairwomen.

Skilled workers are in constantly increasing demand in our growing economy. Opportunities for skilled workers exist in every state and city in the nation and, thus, if a married craftswoman's husband changes jobs and must relocate, she need have little or no fear of finding employment in her new place of residence. In some crafts, the demand far exceeds the supply; as a result, the skilled workers in these occupations may earn more than many professional workers.

Realistically, however, you must accept the fact that attitudes and prejudices often take long to change, and sexist discrimination has been especially strong and pervasive in the skilled occupations. Although you are very much needed, there is no welcome mat out for you here. However, the law is on your side and so, if you are qualified, employers are required to hire you and, therefore, can be compelled to do so.

It is well to note here that some of the best opportunities for craftswomen are in those trades where you can become self-employed, such as appliance servicewoman, automobile mechanic, carpenter, maintenance electrician, painter and paperhanger, television and radio service technician and watch repairwoman. Self-employment in these trades is something to which you should give serious consideration.

If you have the necessary aptitudes and would like to enter any one of the crafts, don't let sexist prejudices deter you. Get the required training and use your manual skills to push open the doors to the manual occupations.

For further information about the skilled occupations, read this writer's *Your Career if You're Not Going to College* (Julian Messner, revised edition, 1971). You might also like to write to the Bureau of Apprenticeship and Training, Manpower Administration, U.S. Department of Labor, Washington, D.C. 20210, and the American Federation of Labor–Congress of Industrial Organizations (AFL-CIO), 815 16th St. N.W., Washington, D.C. 20006.

es for part-time employment. Married women with children
ner home obligations may find the part-time work programs
nswer to their problems. The Atomic Energy Commission,
eterans' Administration and the Departments of Agricul-
Labor, Transportation, Housing and Urban Development
Health, Education and Welfare are among the agencies
n have part-time clerical and/or professional positions open
omen. For specific information about available positions,
ct the personnel department of any of the aforementioned
ies nearest your home.

t as things have been changing in the civilian sector of the
al government, so too there are changes and expanding op-
nities for women in the military sector. *Servicewomen* may
rise to the highest ranks.

June, 1970, President Richard M. Nixon elevated two
en *colonels* to the rank of *U.S. Army brigadier general.* Prior
s, no woman had ever risen higher than colonel. Elizabeth
oisington, director of the Women's Army Corps (WAC)
August, 1966, became brigadier general in charge of 1,000
rs and 12,000 enlisted women. Anna McCabe Hays, chief
e Army Nurse Corps since September, 1967, was raised to
dier general, supervising over 7,000 professional nurses and
0 paraprofessionals. General Hoisington and General Hays
became the first women generals in the history of the U.S.
y.

ter two women were appointed *U.S. Air Force generals,*
in April, 1972, Captain Alene Bertha Duerk was elevated
e rank of U.S. Navy admiral to become the Navy's first
an admiral.

the spring of 1972, on the thirtieth birthday of the WACs,
U.S. Army began to train women in the drill instructor
ol at Fort Jackson, South Carolina. The school is known to be
ed, and this was the first time women were accepted into
become *WAC DIs (drill instructors).*

Chapter 11

THE GOVERNMENT SERVICES

"YOU need a good rich uncle to get a good job," a cynical college senior recently said to me.

Well, I do not agree with the cynical senior on this point, but
nonetheless it happens that you do have a "good rich uncle"—
your Uncle Sam—and he needs qualified females to fill positions
of many sorts. There were more than 2,500,000 *federal government employees* in 1970. Of this number, about 700,000 were
women and over 1,800,000 were men; percentage-wise, about
28 per cent were women and 72 per cent were men.

The federal government employs women in just about every
field of occupational endeavor, from accounting and archaeology
to space exploration and zoology. However, in 1970, 77 per cent
of the women, white-collar workers were in the lowest-grade
positions (grades GS-1 through GS-6), whereas only 1 per cent
of the women were in the highest-grade positions (grades GS-13
and above).

Many efforts are being made to upgrade female federal *civil
service employees.* The U.S. Civil Service Commission established
the Federal Women's Program to help in the implementation of
the government's equal opportunity policy. Information about
this program and opportunities for women in federal service may
be obtained from Helene S. Markoff, Director, Federal Women's

Program, U.S. Civil Service Commission, 1900 E St. N.W., Room 7530, Washington, D.C. 20415.

There are many formerly male-only federal government positions which are now open to women. Law enforcement in the federal government has gone "co-ed," and women are now serving as *armed security guards* in many government installations. The U.S. Postal Service has appointed *women guards* to the Postal Security Force to help reduce mail thefts.

Women are now being hired to work as *mail carriers*. They must have the same physical qualifications as male applicants, and these include the ability to lift seventy pounds. The Postal Service now also has women enrolled in the "Management Associate" program. If you would like to work for the Postal Service as a letter carrier or in any other capacity, write to the U.S. Postal Service, Executive Functions Group, Washington, D.C. 20260.

In May, 1972, L. Patrick Gray, then Acting Director of the Federal Bureau of Investigation, abandoned the FBI's long-standing male-only policy. In July, 1972, the first two women were sworn in to undergo training as *FBI special agents*, or *G-women*. The intensive fourteen-week training course which they had to complete, as all FBI agents must, included firearms training in the use of a .38 caliber revolver, shotgun and rifle. If you are interested in further information about the position of FBI special agent or other career opportunities with the FBI, write to the Federal Bureau of Investigation, U.S. Department of Justice, Washington, D.C. 20535.

The Bureau of Customs of the U.S. Department of Treasury has begun to appoint qualified women to the following positions traditionally occupied by men only: *customs inspector, customs patrol officer, customs security officer, import specialist* and *special agent*. Further information about these positions may be obtained by writing to the Commissioner of Customs, Bureau of

Customs, U.S. Department of the Treasury, V 20226.

The U.S. Department of State, in the sum tablished a full-time office to improve the stat is now actively recruiting women for such trad positions as *security officers* and *couriers*. In nities are opening up for women as *Foreign* you would like to serve with the Foreign Serv States of America, write for details to the Bo for the Foreign Service, U.S. Department of S D.C. 20520.

Employment opportunities for female accou *Revenue agents* in the Internal Revenue Servi to be good for the remainder of the 1970s. Unt were employed as *criminal investigators* by tl positions, which require the carrying of fire women on the same basis as men. For add about IRS positions, write to the College R nator, Internal Revenue Service, U.S. Depart sury, Washington, D.C. 20224.

See Chapter 9 for information on employ for females in male-dominated occupations ir tion Administration.

A group of female federal government em gether during the summer of 1968 and for ployed Women, Inc. Its major purposes are end sex discrimination in employment in the and "to increase job opportunities for women service and to further the potential of all wo ment." Further information about FEW may to the Membership Chairman, Federally Emp 487 National Press Building, Washington, D

A number of government agencies offer v

The Women's Army Corps announced during the summer of 1972 that it would probably double in size in five years and that WACs would hold just about any assignment, including those formerly considered male-only, with the exception of combat duty. Until recently, WACs performed mainly clerical and administrative jobs, but the time has come for them to be serving alongside of men in such traditionally male jobs as *missile-repair crewmen, radar technicians, electronics specialists* and *heavy equipment operators.*

You may find your place among the many expanding career opportunities in the military services. To get the latest details about military opportunities for career training and experience, write to the U.S. Department of Defense, Washington, D.C. 20301.

The states and cities throughout the nation in their totality employ even more government workers than does the federal government. Most employees in the police and fire protection services are employed by state and local government agencies.

Alice Stebbins Wells in 1910 became the first *policewoman* in the United States. She had been a welfare worker in Los Angeles, California, and was convinced that women are better equipped than men to serve as *police officers* doing protective service and preventive work with women and children. Through her efforts the basis for the juvenile bureaus and crime prevention bureaus of our modern police departments was established.

Although more than half a century has passed since the days of Alice Wells, women represent only a tiny percentage of the total number of police officers. Of approximately 330,000 police officers employed by local police departments in 1970, only about 6,000 (less than 2 per cent) were women. Until quite recently, the vast majority of these policewomen were assigned either to desk jobs or to work with juveniles. Now, however, not only are police departments adding more women to their staffs, but additionally policewomen are being assigned to tasks which have been traditionally for policemen only. Among these tasks

211

are street patrol duties, investigation of crimes, driving squad cars and answering radio calls, particularly where the latter involve family squabbles.

Patrolwomen are pounding their beats in Washington, D.C., New York City, Indianapolis, Miami, Peoria, St. Louis and other cities throughout the country. Most of them are part of experimental programs designed to determine whether these women can handle highly dangerous situations. Interestingly, the women are proving themselves well able to cope where violence is involved. With the passage of time, surely more policewomen will be assigned to challenging, dangerous duties traditionally considered the work of policemen only. Some are already serving as *detectives* or *plainclotheswomen* on hazardous assignments. A small number are *traffic policewomen.*

Requirements for becoming a policewoman differ from city to city. However, if you hope to advance from patrolwoman to *police sergeant, lieutenant* and *captain,* a college degree with a major in law enforcement including courses in psychology, sociology and minority-group relations is highly desirable. Physical stamina, agility, alertness and a great deal of intestinal fortitude are needed for those who aspire to police careers. The employment future appears to be very favorable for qualified women who desire such careers.

Policewomen have their own association, the International Association of Women Police, 100 N. LaSalle St., Chicago, Ill. 60602. There is also the Women's Correctional Association (affiliated with the American Correctional Association), c/o Secretary-Treasurer, Marilyn Davenport, New Jersey Reformatory for Women, Clinton, N.J. 08809, which includes among its members *superintendents, wardens* and others working with female offenders.

The number of female *firefighters* is negligible. This is one male-only occupation which may remain so for many years to come, owing to the uniquely difficult physical demands of the work. The average weight of a firefighter's fire-protective equipment exceeds sixty pounds. Add to this the weight of the hose to be dragged into a burning building or of the fire victim to be carried out of the building, and you have a great deal of weight to carry. But perhaps YOU can do it.

Women could, of course, serve as firefighters in the communications (fire alarm) section of the local fire department. Perhaps you have the physical capacity to perform the actual firefighting functions. If you do and if you would like to become a firefighter, go ahead and apply to your local fire department or civil service commission, and good luck to you! You might also like to write for further information to the International Association of Fire Fighters, 905 16th St. N.W., Washington, D.C. 20006.

For information about nontraditional or traditional employment opportunities for women with your state or local government, write to your state civil service commission located in your state capital or your municipal civil service commission, often located in the local city hall.

Politics is defined as the science or art of political government. There are women in politics on all levels of government—federal, state and local. Most *politicians,* however, are men. Women traditionally have served as volunteers, ringing doorbells and distributing leaflets to publicize the candidates of their choice, rather than being candidates themselves.

Unprecedented political activism was demonstrated by women at both the Democratic and Republican presidential conventions in the summer of 1972. At both conventions, women were present as delegates in greater numbers than ever before. At the Democratic convention, the name of a woman, Shirley Chisholm of New York, was placed in nomination for the position of *president,* and the name of another woman, Frances "Sissy" Farenthold of Texas, was placed in nomination for the position of *vice-president.* However, the number of women who hold elective office on local or national levels, as *councilwomen, assembly-*

213

women, state senators, mayors, governors, congresswomen, U.S. senators or other *elected officials,* is still quite small.

Congresswoman Shirley Chisholm (Democrat, New York), who had been the only black woman in the U.S. House of Representatives, was joined by two other black women in January, 1973, in the 93rd Congress—Yvonne Brathwaite Burke (Democrat, California), from the 37th Congressional District of Los Angeles, and Barbara Jordan (Democrat, Texas), from the 18th Congressional District of Houston. Congresswoman Burke had served previously as an *assemblywoman* and Congresswoman Jordan as a *state senator.*

The only woman in the U.S. Senate in the 92nd Congress, Senator Margaret Chase Smith (Republican, Maine), who had served with distinction for four terms, was defeated by a young male opponent in the elections of November, 1972, in her bid for a fifth term.

The nonpartisan National Women's Political Caucus was founded in July, 1971. If you would like to know more about the N.W.P.C. and perhaps to join it, write to the National Women's Political Caucus, 1302 18th St. N.W., Washington, D.C. 20036.

The Eagleton Institute of Politics at Rutgers University has a "Center for the American Woman and Politics." This center is nonpartisan and was established in 1971 "dedicated to the study of American women and politics and to promoting the full and active involvement of women in American public life." For details about this center and its programs, write to the Eagleton Center for the American Woman and Politics, Rutgers University, The State University of New Jersey, Wood Lawn, Neilson Campus, New Brunswick, N.J. 08901.

Of all the nontraditional jobs for women, the most nontraditional of all is the presidency of the United States, for a woman has never served in that office.

There are many who think that Representative Shirley Chisholm is the first woman to have run for president. This is not so.

It will probably surprise you to learn that a woman ran for the highest office in the land more than one hundred years ago. Her name was Victoria C. Woodhull, and she ran as a nominee of the Equal Rights Party in 1872.

Increasing numbers of women are holding important government positions and winning elective offices on all levels of government. The day may be sooner than you think for a woman to become *president of the United States*. The next "Victoria" may be victorious and—who knows—she may be YOU!

Chapter 12

STAMP OUT
OUTMODED STEREOTYPES

WHEN Dr. Samuel Johnson was asked, "Which is more intelligent, man or woman?", he replied, "Which man, and which woman?"

Right on—and bravo for Dr. Johnson for an excellent reply.

In striving to banish stereotypes, women are not saying that they are smarter than men or that men are stupider than women. That is utter nonsense. People are individuals.

Women Are People

As people, some women are more intelligent than most men and some men are more intelligent than most women. Some individuals, female and male alike, are above average in intelligence; others are of below average intelligence; and most have average intelligence.

Each of us, female and male, has God-given potentials. We differ individually in the kind and quantity of potentials we possess. Some of us have more than others of certain potentials and some have less than others, but none of us uses anywhere near the amount of potential which the good Lord gave to us. This is sad. Women dream dreams just as men do, and all people —women and men—should have the opportunity to realize their dreams.

Intelligent women and intelligent men can and should work

alongside of each other in fields which are presently male-dominated, not to compete with each other in an attempt to prove who is more intelligent, but to complement each other, thus doubling the intelligence applied to a specific task and accomplishing together what could not be accomplished individually.

Do you have the intelligence and ability to become a scientist or engineer or lawyer or internist or business executive or whatever other nontraditionalist you wish to become? Well, then, go ahead and do so!

Stereotypes are contrary to the facts and to nature's endowment of women with a variety of mental abilities and aptitudes. Let's erase the stereotypic images and myths which society has for all too long imposed upon us.

About 32,000,000 women were working at paid employment in mid-1973. Most worked because of economic necessity. Others worked to raise their standard of living. Some worked for self-fulfillment. It is anticipated that, by 1980, about 38,000,000 women will be in the labor force and most will be married women. Nine out of every ten women will work at paid employment at some time during their lives.

Paid employment is an important aspect of a woman's life. Since homemaking is no longer either a full-time or lifetime occupation even if you are married and have a family, you will in all likelihood be spending many years at your job. You can by wise career choices make these gratifying, fulfilling and financially rewarding years.

If You Believe You Can Achieve, You Can!
Much self-fulfillment and financial reward await you in the nontraditional fields. Do you have the intestinal fortitude which every female needs if she is to enter these fields? It takes a good deal of courage and inner strength to prepare for and enter a nontraditional occupation and not permit others to scare you away from such a course of action.

NONTRADITIONAL CAREERS FOR WOMEN

Do you have the "guts" enough to do so?

If you have confidence in yourself, if you believe you can achieve, you can!

If you enter a field where the percentage of women is small, you will be like an explorer seeking new worlds. There will be many challenges ahead and barriers to hurdle. Despite federal legislation against sexist discrimination, all too often this legislation is being circumvented, and instead, in far too many places, there is still mere lip service and tokenism. It may not be easy for you, but happiness does not come from doing what is easy. Happiness comes from facing up to challenges and overcoming them.

Although it may not be easy for you to gain entry into many of the currently predominantly male occupations, remember that it is much easier for you than it was for all the women who came before you, for the women about whom you have read in this book and for the thousands of other women now working in nontraditional fields. They paved the way for you, and your occupational pathways are, therefore, smoother. It was difficult for those who came before you, but it was and continues to be very, very much worth it! And, remember too, the winds of change are in your favor.

You may encounter a barrage of criticism as you prepare to enter certain nontraditional careers, and these barbs may come from women as well as men. Those who do not have the ability, ambition and courage enough to train for and enter nontraditional fields may do all within their power to discourage you from doing so. Don't let them discourage you! Learn to ignore them!

Ambitionless, fearful and/or insecure people do not achieve very much and, often enviously, do not want others to achieve. Do not let them prevent you from achieving all you can! Insecure, unsuccessful people will feel threatened by you and may do all within their power to prevent you from achieving your objectives. Don't let them. Don't let yourself suffer from someone else's fears, insecurities, inability and lack of ambition. That's their problem; don't let them make it yours. You will surely meet secure, successful people—male as well as female—who will help you along your pathway to success in a nontraditional occupation.

Don't listen to those who say, "You can't"; say, "I can." Perhaps *they* can't; *you* can! You have a brain—use it!

So many of the nontraditional women I have known have had their personal experiences with those who tried to discourage them. They all wisely and happily ignored the discouragers.

When A.Z., for example, entered college as a "pre-med" major, an unambitious relative of similar age laughed and poked fun at her and did all she could to dissuade A.Z. from becoming a medical doctor. A.Z. ignored her relative. When A.Z. later became a physician and opened her own office, this same relative demanded free medical attention, saying, "I encouraged you to go to medical school. If not for me, you wouldn't be a doctor. Show you're grateful, and give me free service."

If you decide to enter the very male-dominated skilled trades, there are those who may make derogatory remarks about your femininity. They probably envy your courage. So ignore their remarks and enjoy your work!

Remember this—when your head sticks out above the crowd (and it does so when you are a nontraditionalist), there are those jealous people who will throw tomatoes at you. Well, then, convert a negative act into a positive one. Catch the tomatoes, make tomato soup out of them and have a delicious, nutritious meal!

Eliminate Stereotypical Thinking
Too much of female intelligence has for too long gone to waste. Out with stereotypical thinking! Let's get on with the important tasks of eradicating poverty, abolishing urban blight, purging pollution from our environment, helping parents to rear well-adjusted children, easing the suffering of the elderly and the

219

ill and conquering cancer, heart disease, mental illness and all the other ills which ravage the human body and soul.

There is much to be done to improve our troubled world, and it can be done better and faster by intelligent, concerned women and men *working together,* not *in competition* with each other but *in cooperation* with each other.

Millions of jobs are involved to accomplish these and many other important tasks. Jobs have no gender. The modern world has no room for antiquated sex-role stereotypes. There should be no sexism in reverse either. Male occupational stereotypes are as outmoded as female ones. There is no reason why a man cannot be a competent nurse or telephone operator or secretary or member of any other so-called female-only occupations.

Let male and female energies, intelligence and talents be pooled into positive, productive channels to help produce a better, more wholesome world.

Traditional sexist barriers are being battered down, but many employers are still doing all they can (and probably will continue for quite some time) to circumvent the law. A great deal has yet to be done to strengthen and enforce anti-discrimination legislation.

Those of you who will be entering nontraditional occupations have additional work ahead of you—namely, to continue and win the battles for equal educational opportunities with men in apprenticeships, vocational institutions, colleges and universities and all other institutions of learning; for equal pay with men for equal work; for equal promotional opportunities on the job to permit qualified women to rise to the highest levels of their abilities; and for the establishment by government and other agencies of subsidized day care centers for children to enable mothers who wish and/or need to go to work to be able to do their jobs free of worry, knowing that their children are receiving adequate, competent care.

New and expanding opportunities are opening up to you in

ever so many nontraditional fields. There is collective potential for millions of pleasurable and profitable employment opportunities for women in these fields. Women's underutilized and untapped talents are needed in today's troubled world. Womanpower is needed to ease manpower shortages. The good Lord gave you intelligence, abilities, special aptitudes and inclinations. Don't waste them!

Space limitations have not permitted a discussion of job-seeking and job-finding techniques in this book. If you would like information about the latter, read this writer's *Your Career if You're Not Going to College* (Julian Messner, revised edition, 1971).

In our great democracy, you now have the opportunity to develop your talents and intellect to the fullest of your capabilities and to pursue your goals uninhibited and unlimited by outmoded stereotypes. Focus your determination and drive upon the nontraditional occupations. Much gratification and fulfillment await you if you do.

So proceed and make your best possible contribution to yourself, your family, your community and your country.

You can be totally feminine and vocationally fulfilled in the nontraditional fields for females. Go to it; Godspeed and good luck to you!

SUGGESTED FURTHER READINGS

Throughout this book, many sources of further information are mentioned. If you would like to read more about a specific career, you may write to any one or more of these sources, according to your interests, and you will probably receive a variety of pamphlets and other career materials. Additionally, it is suggested that you write for the latest publications and have your name placed on the mailing list of the Women's Bureau, U.S. Department of Labor, Washington, D.C. 20210.

Until recently, little was written on the subject of nontraditional careers for women. This is the first and, thus far, the only book which covers the gamut of nontraditional careers for women. The following recently published books concern a specific nontraditional career, and they merit reading, particularly if your interest lies in the career which is the subject of one or more of these books:

Brownmiller, Susan, *Shirley Chisholm.* New York: Doubleday and Co., Inc., 1970.

Burt, Olive, *Physician to the World: Esther Pohl Lovejoy.* New York: Julian Messner, 1973.

Conn, Frances G., *Ida Tarbell, Muckraker.* New York: Thomas Nelson, Inc., 1972.

Fleming, Alice, *Alice Freeman Palmer: Pioneer College President.* Englewood Cliffs, N.J.: Prentice-Hall, Inc., 1970.

Golde, Peggy, *Women in the Field: Anthropological Experiences.* Chicago: Aldine Publishing Co., 1970.

Heiman, Grover, Jr., and Myers, Virginia H., *Careers for Women in Uniform.* Philadelphia: J. B. Lippincott Co., 1971.

Marks, Geoffrey, and Beatty, William K., *Women in White:*

Their Role as Doctors Through the Ages. New York: Charles Scribner's Sons, 1972.

Myers, Elisabeth P., *Madam Secretary: Frances Perkins.* New York: Julian Messner, 1972.

Noble, Iris, *Cameras and Courage: Margaret Bourke-White.* New York: Julian Messner, 1973.

ABOUT THE AUTHOR

SARAH SPLAVER is a noted guidance consultant and counseling psychologist. She holds a Master of Arts degree from Teachers College, Columbia University, and a Doctor of Philosophy degree from New York University. She served for several years as a high school Director of Guidance. She is nationally and internationally well known as the originator of the socioguidrama, a group guidance technique used as a means of helping young people with their problems.

Dr. Splaver is licensed as a registered psychologist by the Department of Education of the State of New York. She has served as a consultant on psychological and guidance projects to the U. S. Department of Health, Education and Welfare; U. S. Defense Department; Department of the Army; New York Life Insurance Company; International Business Machines Corp., and various other organizations. She has counseled thousands of college-bound and non-collegebound young people and adults. As a consultant, she also works on computerized guidance programs.

Her articles on guidance, psychology and career information have appeared in professional journals and in other publications. She has authored dozens of *Occupational Abstracts,* prepared the *Guide to Career Literature* for the New York Life Insurance Company's Career Information Service, and has written many books and playlets in the field of guidance and psychology. She has lectured at conferences, young people's gatherings and parent-teacher and other meetings. She is the former Director of *Guidance Exchange.*

Dr. Splaver is a Fellow of the International Council of Psychologists and a Life Member of the American Personnel and Guidance Association. Among the other professional organizations in which she holds membership are the National Vocational Guidance Association, American School Counselor Association, American Psychological Association, Institutes of Religion and Health, American Association for the Advancement of Science and the Authors Guild.

224